BLUE NOTE

THE ALBUM COVER ART

EDITED BY GRAHAM MARSH, FELIX CROMEY, AND GLYN CALLINGHAM

Foreword by Horace Silver

CHRONICLE BOOKS · SAN FRANCISCO

FIRST PUBLISHED IN THE U.S. BY CHRONICLE BOOKS.

COPYRIGHT 1991 BY COLLINS & BROWN.
ALL RIGHTS RESERVED.
NO PART OF THIS BOOK MAY BE REPRODUCED WITHOUT
WRITTEN PERMISSION FROM THE PUBLISHER.

PRINTED IN HONG KONG

COVER DESIGN: KAREN SMIDTH

LIBRARY OF CONGRESS CATALOGING-IN-PUBLICATION DATA AVAILABLE.

ISBN: 0-8118-0036-9

10 9 8 7 6

CHRONICLE BOOKS
275 FIFTH STREET
SAN FRANCISCO, CA 94103

ACKNOWLEDGEMENTS

Thanks go to several cool people for making this book possible.
Especially Alfred Lion, Francis Wolff, Rudy Van Gelder, Reid Miles,
Ruth Lion, Art Blakey, Horace Silver and a host of Blue Note
Musicians without whom it would not exist. And Ann Barr, Mark
Collins and Gabrielle Townsend who bought it.

Also the following must get theirs . . .
EMI, London
Blue Note Records, New York
John Jack/Cadillac Music
Nicola Jeal
Beth Aves
Geoff Dann/Sleeve Photography
Wendy Furness
Ray Smith, Bob Glass, Mike Doyle and Nick Easterbrook
at Ray's Jazz Shop
Michael Cuscuna
Michel Ruppli
Bruce Lundvall
Sam the Cat
Down Beat Magazine
Sarah Bloxham
Kate, Ruth and Hannah Sutcliffe
Brooks Brothers
Mike Gavin
Ian Shipley
Denis and Pauline Cromey
Wire Magazine
The Crew from the Island
Ashton Baldwin
Mike and Jo Bell
Laurie, Mark, Alan and Jon at Honest Jon's
John Clarke
Michael Dean
Maurice White
Andy Titcombe
Esquire Magazine
The South Bank Show/LWT
John Hermansader
Tom Hannan
Ronnie Brathwaite
Jean-Pierre Leloir
Larry Miller
Harold Feinstein
Paula Donohue
Jim Marshall
T. Fujiyama
A. Miyashita
T. Tanaka
Forlenza Venosa Design Associates
William Connors
Buck Hoeffler
George Wright
Bill Penny
Charles Reilly
Quantum
Andy Warhol

CONTENTS

FOREWORD

"Blue Note Records were very meticulous in every aspect
of their production: they used the best vinyl, they
paid for rehearsals and when I asked to be in on the other
parts of my album Alfred Lion (the label's founder)
gave me every opportunity. A lot of musicians in those days
worked very hard to make good music and once the
music was done, they let Alfred Lion go with the rest of it.
One day I went to Alfred and said, I want to sit down
with you and look at the pictures you want to use and pick
them together and check the sleeve notes before
you print them. He agreed to that, and so I had input over a
lot of things the other guys didn't bother with.
I learnt a lot from that, and what I learnt about making a
record I learnt from Alfred Lion.
   I don't have a favourite cover of mine . . . but thinking
back now you know, I kinda like the *Tokyo Blues* cover!"

HORACE SILVER
(Blue Note Recording Star 1952—1979)
Silveto Productions / Emerald Records 1990

THE HISTORY OF
BLUE NOTE RECORDS

1925: Alfred Lion, aged sixteen, experiences Sam Woodyard and his Chocolate Dandies in concert and is profoundly affected by the wonderful music.

1930: Lion makes his first trip to the United States, purchasing over 300 records unavailable in his native Germany.

1938: Lion emigrates to the US, escaping Nazism and embracing Hot Jazz. Attends the legendary Spirituals to Swing concert and is transfixed by boogie-woogie pianists Albert Ammons and Meade Lux Lewis.

1939: Ammons and Lewis are recorded by Lion at an after-hours session. The results are pressed up into fifty twelve-inch discs which soon sell out. The first brochure is produced detailing the label's intent. Sidney Bechet records *Summertime* for Blue Note giving the label a 'hit'.

1941: Francis Wolff, Alfred Lion's associate, joins him from Germany.

1942: Blue Note suspends production for the duration of the war. Lion is drafted into US Army.

1943: The label resumes activities, moving to 767 Lexington Avenue, New York, NY, and during the next four years records small swingtets (comprising seven or eight players).

1948: By this time Blue Note had absorbed the stylistic changes of Bop and was recording the new talents, such as Thelonious Monk, Bud Powell and Fats Navarro.

1951: The year that Blue Note moved from 78s to the ten-inch format, introducing as it did the need for cover art. Paul Bacon, Gil Melle and John Hermansader are the early cover designers.

1953: Gil Melle introduces Lion to Rudy Van Gelder, a recording engineer working from home in Hackensack, New Jersey. It was Van Gelder's ears that helped mould what became known as the 'Blue Note sound'. His attention to details, such as the audibility of the hi-hat cymbal, gave the records their definition and dimensional warmth.

1954: The Jazz Messengers are born (including Horace Silver and Art Blakey) heralding a new era of soulful, swinging and inventive jazz.

1956: Reid Miles begins working with Lion and Wolff as Blue Note's graphic designer. Soon-to-become legendary organist Jimmy Smith is signed to the label, completing the cast, as Michael Cuscuna described it, with Lion, Wolff, Blakey, Silver, Van Gelder and Reid Miles.

1958: Fledgling 'Star', Andy Warhol, draws a reclining woman motif for the covers of Kenny Burrell's *Blue Lights* Volumes 1 and 2.

1959: Blue Note, with new A&R man Ike Quebec, move recordings to Van Gelder's new studio at Englewood Cliffs, NJ.

1963: Ike Quebec succeeded by Duke Pearson.

1964: Blue Note have two hit albums in the grooving *Song For My Father* by Horace Silver and *The Sidewinder* by Lee Morgan.

1965: The recording giant Liberty makes Blue Note chiefs Alfred Lion and Francis Wolff an offer to sell out. The two were becoming exhausted by their diligence to the label and accepted the offer.

1967: Alfred Lion quits Blue Note due to health problems. The label no longer has Reid Miles as graphic designer and the visual changes become disturbingly obvious.

1971: Francis Wolff dies. The label moves towards fusion and continues to have hits.

1975: A re-issue programme continues the tradition of Blue Note's heyday, with classic albums made available again. This particular programme survives until 1981.

1985: Blue Note is fully revived by Bruce Lundvall and Michael Cuscuna, at Capitol Records, with a comprehensive re-issue catalogue of old classics and previously unheard gems. New artists are signed, as well as new albums from old faces such as McCoy Tyner. The label celebrates with a party at the Town Hall, New York and the whole jamboree is committed to vinyl and video.

1990: Blue Note is afforded space in many surveys of Twentieth Century music, outlining its indelible importance.

Compiled by FELIX CROMEY

A NEW PERSPECTIVE
SLEEVE NOTES FOR REID MILES

Reid Miles designed almost 500 Blue Note record sleeves during a period of some fifteen years: a canon of work so individually styled, that a Reid Miles sleeve was as recognizable as the trumpet timbre of Miles Davis or the plaintive phrasing of Billie Holiday.

As Blue Note embraced the musical changes of its recording artists, so Reid Miles caught the slipstream creating sleeves that transcended the mugshots and mysticism of other genres' sleeves.

Whether cropping the photographs (taken by label boss Francis Wolff) to minimal proportions or finding a funky typeface, Reid Miles made the cover sound like it knew what lay in store for the listener: an abstract design hinting at innovations, cool strides for cool notes, the symbolic implications of typeface and tones.

Though commercial artists such as Harold Feinstein and Andy Warhol were commissioned by Blue Note, it wasn't until Reid Miles took over as the in-house designer that the label could boast of a visual identity to match the 'Blue Note sound' created by Rudy Van Gelder and Alfred Lion. Though Miles considered the Warhol sleeves for Kenny Burrell's records to be wonderful, especially in their graphic simplicity, his own work still gives him a sense of tremendous pride. As with any innovator, Reid Miles could be found ahead of the pack; stylistic changes made in his work consistently re-invented themselves to prevent any sense of déjà vu.

In 1958 the sleeve for *Peckin' Time* by Hank Mobley showed the album's acetate protective sleeve, handles and fortified corners clearly visible, with the main session details printed on the outside. In 1959 this was stripped down to a card folder for *Jackie's Bag* by Jackie McLean, tied in the centre by a coloured thong, with the session details printed on a label. A visual pun appears: Art Taylor is listed as Art Sailor but this is poorly concealed by a series of typed Xs.

Miles considers this sleeve to be 'an incredible concept for the time'. The rakish angle of the stamp bearing the album's title combined with the humour create an informality that would only re-occur in the 'Sgt. Pepper' period.

As the label moved into the Sixties, Miles found the inspiration for what he considers his best work for Blue Note. The changes in the consumer world brought about an era of design classics, amongst them the E-Type Jaguar sports car. With its reptilian headlights and elongated, curvaceous wings it provided the perfect foil to frame the relaxed features of Donald Byrd. The album was titled *A New Perspective* which was triumphantly reiterated by the foreshortening effect of Miles' camera position. The fine lines combine to give a smoothness redolent of skin, not steel.

Miles' needle, despite this success, did not stick in this stylistic groove. In 1964 he produced the ultimate pared down graphics of *In 'n Out* for Joe Henderson. The typeface swerved to suit the implications of the title whilst the artist's photograph, so often abbreviated, became the definitive punctuation mark forming, as it did, the dot of the *I*.

However, Miles was to return to the car motif, almost a year to the day from the highway codes of *In 'n Out*, for Stanley Turrentine's *Joyride*. Perhaps this is the culmination of the design traits most associated with Blue Note through the Fifties and Sixties. The incorporation of the musician's face, two typefaces, a car and the abstract textures in equal measures forms a startling image. The headlight cowling puts the musician in context vis-à-vis the title; however, the swirl of undergrowth and the comparative sharpness of the musician's reflection suggest the capturing of a fleeting moment suspended in this timeless composition.

Whilst Contemporary had William Claxton, with his photographic eye for 'la mode' of the modalist, and Clef had the unmistakable, quirky wit of David Stone Martin's much-copied linear drawings, Blue Note had Reid Miles. Whatever was Hank Mobley's next groove was Reid Miles' next move!

FELIX CROMEY

NO ROOM FOR SQUARES

Consider the irony — the button-down shirt, which came to symbolize all that was hip about the Blue Note musicians, was originally English. Polo players at the turn of the century were seen by John Brooks, of Brooks Brothers, to fasten their collars with buttons to keep them from snapping in their faces. Brooks, no novice in such matters, took the idea back to New York and turned it into standard issue Ivy League.

This piece of sartorial history was of no concern to us, however; the mere fact that Hank Mobley, Sonny Rollins, Art Blakey and other Blue Note luminaries were photographed wearing these shirts, on their respective album covers, was endorsement enough.

Now I'm sure to those musicians it was just another clean shirt, but in the early Sixties, unless your taste was for home-grown, the importance of being imported applied to the clothes as much as to the records. While Modern Jazz was required listening, the desired look for any self-respecting hipster was American Ivy League.

Time not going to clubs, listening to records or just hanging out was reserved for tracking down those essential imported threads. Black and white photographs on the backs of record sleeves, copies of *Esquire* and *Down Beat* magazines helped bring the details into focus.

It was an obsession; a friend of mine was not a happy person until he owned a striped button-down identical to the Shirt *Big* John Patton wore on the sleeve of *The Way I Feel*. Eventually the obsession turned into some kind of eternal quest to score the correct items of clothing on the menu — narrow lapels to go, hold the double-breasted!

Let me tell you what we looked like. You can probably get an argument about it, but the generally accepted shirt was either plain blue or white Oxford cloth button-down, a close second was the tab collar. The necktie was knitted, narrow, very black and made by Rooster. A leather or webbing belt held up the trousers of a three-button, natural-shouldered, half-lined raised-seam suit, with the inevitable six-inch hooked vent. The purist suit was in tan needlecord, or olive or dark blue cotton. At the bottom of the narrow, plain-front trousers, beneath the one-and-a-half-inch cuffs, was a pair of long wing-tip brogues or beef-roll loafers with the lowest heels you've ever seen.

The Mecca for most of these ready made American clothes was the late, great store — Austins', situated on Shaftesbury Avenue in London. A visit to which severely dented the hard-earned folding.

Today, by way of compensation, with original Blue Note records fetching prices that Sotheby's would be proud of, you can still buy a Brooks Brothers' button-down shirt for about forty-eight dollars — plus the airfare to New York.

GRAHAM MARSH

9

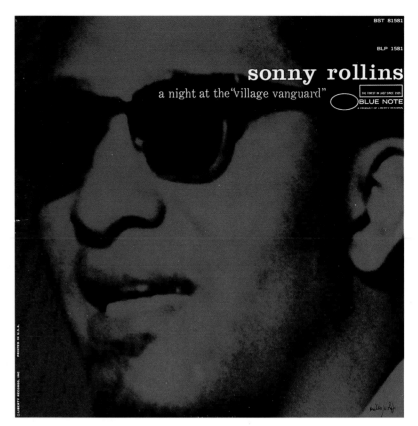

A NIGHT AT THE "VILLAGE VANGUARD"   1581
Artist SONNY ROLLINS
Cover Design by REID MILES
Cover Photo by FRANCIS WOLFF

"They were sure that with these new
artists they were introducing, so many of them
were leaders for the first time, so
maybe the public in Harlem knew about them,
but across the country they didn't . . .
and they felt it was very important to put these
mens' photos as prominently as
possible on the covers and they got a lot of flak
from distributors across the country
who felt a pretty girl would have been better."
RUTH LION

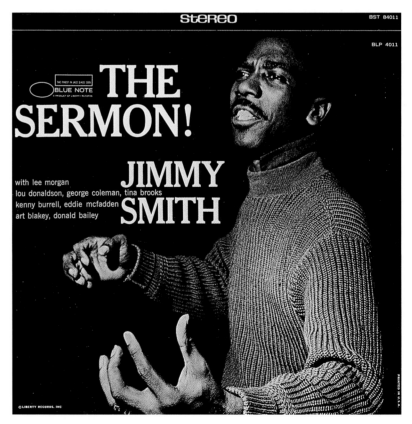

THE SERMON!   4011
Artist JIMMY SMITH
Cover Design by REID MILES
Cover Photo by FRANCIS WOLFF

Opposite: BLUE TRAIN 1577 Artist JOHN COLTRANE Cover Design by REID MILES Cover Photo by FRANCIS WOLFF

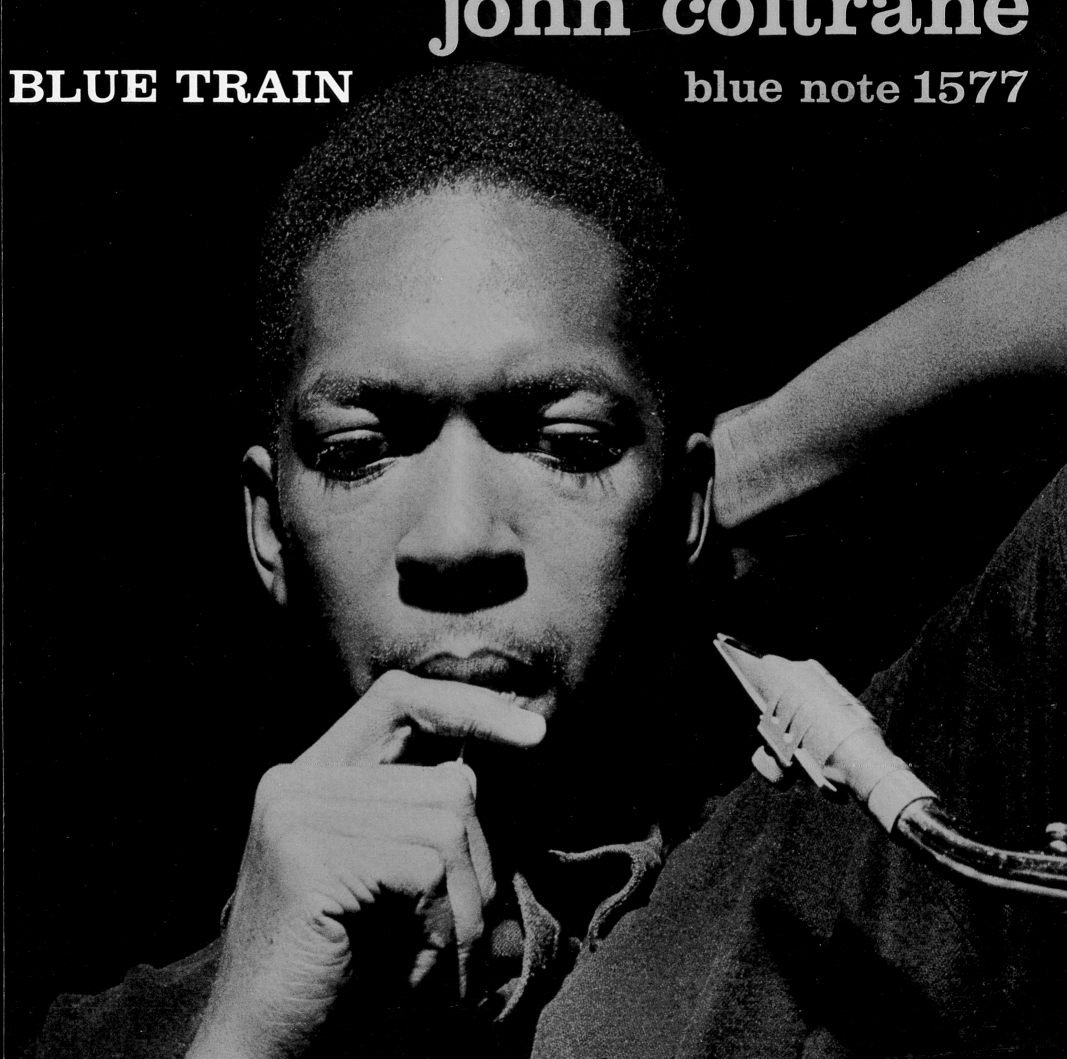

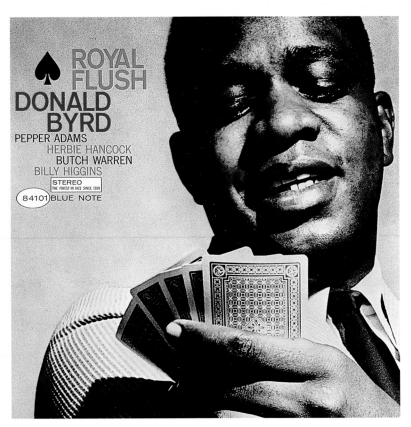

ROYAL FLUSH 4101
Artist DONALD BYRD
Cover Design by REID MILES
Cover Photo by FRANCIS WOLFF

'THE WAY I FEEL' 4174
Artist JOHN PATTON
Cover Design by REID MILES
Cover Photo by FRANCIS WOLFF

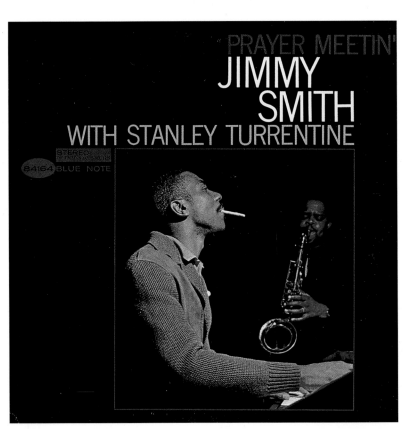

PRAYER MEETIN' 4164
Artist JIMMY SMITH
Cover Design by REID MILES
Cover Photo by FRANCIS WOLFF

DOIN' THE THING 4076
Artist HORACE SILVER
Cover Photo by JIM MARSHALL

Opposite: POINT OF DEPARTURE 4167 Artist ANDREW HILL Cover Design by REID MILES Cover Photo by REID MILES

STEREO
THE FINEST IN JAZZ SINCE 1939
84167 BLUE NOTE

POINT OF DEPARTURE
ANDREW HILL
KENNY DORHAM / ERIC DOLPHY
JOE HENDERSON / RICHARD DAVIS
ANTHONY WILLIAMS

STEREO
THE FINEST IN JAZZ SINCE 1939

MILES DAVIS VOLUME 1 1501
Artist MILES DAVIS
Cover Design by REID MILES/JOHN HERMANSADER
Cover Photo by FRANCIS WOLFF

MILES DAVIS VOLUME 2 1502
Artist MILES DAVIS
Cover Design by REID MILES/JOHN HERMANSADER
Cover Photo by FRANCIS WOLFF

THE NIGHT OF THE COOKERS VOLUME 1 4207
Artist FREDDIE HUBBARD
Cover Design by REID MILES
Cover Photo by FRANCIS WOLFF

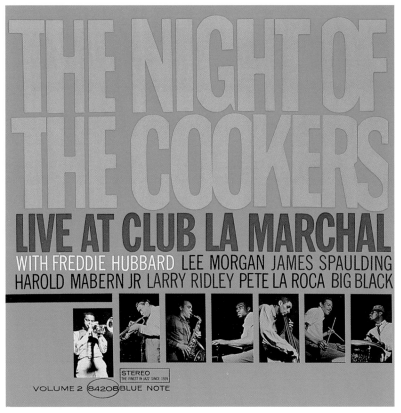

THE NIGHT OF THE COOKERS VOLUME 2 4208
Artist FREDDIE HUBBARD
Cover Design by REID MILES
Cover Photo by FRANCIS WOLFF

Opposite: OUR MAN IN PARIS 4146 Artist DEXTER GORDON Cover Design by REID MILES Cover Photo by FRANCIS WOLFF

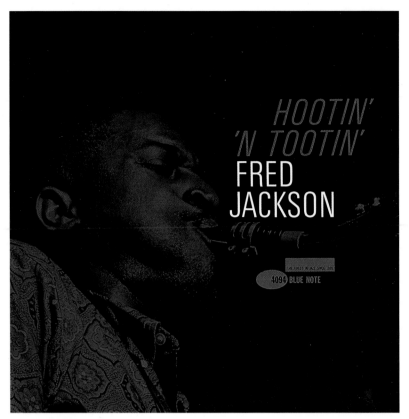

HOOTIN' 'N TOOTIN' 4094
Artist FRED JACKSON
Cover Design by REID MILES
Cover Photo by FRANCIS WOLFF

"I would say that ninety per cent of Frank's photos were taken at the recording sessions. I got the pictures from Frank and I integrated them within the design of the moment."
REID MILES

16

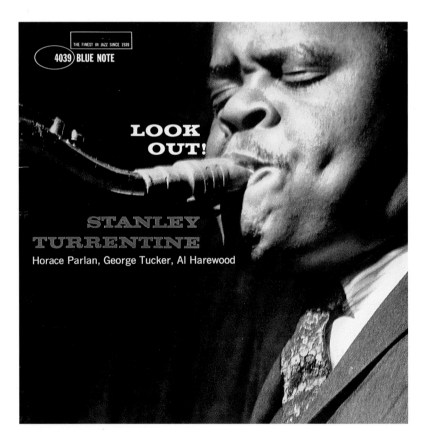

LOOK OUT! 4039
Artist STANLEY TURRENTINE
Cover Design by REID MILES
Cover Photo by FRANCIS WOLFF

Opposite: WORKOUT 4080 Artist HANK MOBLEY Cover Photo by FRANCIS WOLFF

grant green / wynton kelly / paul chambers / philly joe jones

WORKOUT HANK MOBLEY

STEREO
THE FINEST IN JAZZ SINCE 1939

84080 BLUE NOTE

THE THING TO DO 4178
Artist BLUE MITCHELL
Cover Design by REID MILES
Cover Photo by FRANCIS WOLFF

CAPUCHIN SWING 4038
Artist JACKIE McLEAN
Cover Design by REID MILES
Cover Photo by FRANCIS WOLFF

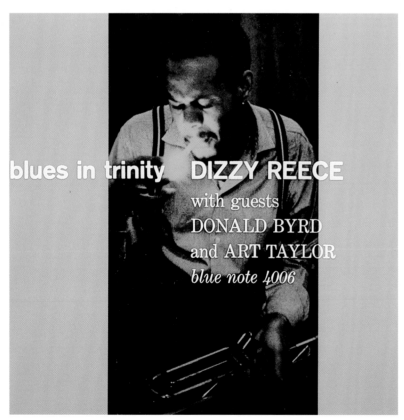

BLUES IN TRINITY 4006
Artist DIZZY REECE
Cover Design by REID MILES
Cover Photo by BILL PENNY

JOHN JENKINS WITH KENNY BURRELL 1573
Artist JOHN JENKINS
Cover Design by TOM HANNAN
Cover Photo by FRANCIS WOLFF

Opposite: SONNY ROLLINS 1542 Artist SONNY ROLLINS Cover Design by REID MILES Cover Photo by FRANCIS WOLFF

SONNY ROLLINS

blue note 81542

THE FABULOUS FATS NAVARRO

blue note 81531 volume 1

THE FABULOUS FATS NAVARRO

blue note 81532 volume 2

THE FABULOUS FATS NAVARRO VOLUME 1 1531
Artist FATS NAVARRO
Cover Design by REID MILES
Cover Photo by FRANCIS WOLFF

THE FABULOUS FATS NAVARRO VOLUME 2 1532
Artist FATS NAVARRO
Cover Design by REID MILES
Cover Photo by FRANCIS WOLFF

BLUE NOTE 1568

HANK MOBLEY

BILL HARDMAN CURTIS PORTER SONNY CLARK PAUL CHAMBERS ART TAYLOR

CLIFFORD BROWN
blue note 1526 memorial album

HANK MOBLEY 1568
Artist HANK MOBLEY
Cover Design by TOM HANNAN
Cover Photo by FRANCIS WOLFF

MEMORIAL ALBUM 1526
Artist CLIFFORD BROWN
Cover Photo by FRANCIS WOLFF

Opposite: J. R. MONTEROSE 1536 Artist J. R. MONTEROSE Cover Design by REID MILES Cover Photo by FRANCIS WOLFF

J. R. MONTEROSE

WITH IRA SULLIVAN/HORACE SILVER/WILBUR WARE/"PHILLY" JOE JONES/BLUE NOTE 1536

GENIUS OF MODERN MUSIC VOLUME 1 1510
Artist THELONIOUS MONK
Cover Design by REID MILES
Cover Photo by FRANCIS WOLFF

GENIUS OF MODERN MUSIC
THELONIOUS MONK

BLP 1510 Vol. 1
'ROUND ABOUT MIDNIGHT
OFF MINOR
RUBY MY DEAR
I MEAN YOU
**APRIL IN PARIS
IN WALKED BUD
THELONIOUS
EPISTROPHY
MISTERIOSO
WELL YOU NEEDN'T
*INTROSPECTION
HUMPH

BLP 1511 Vol. 2
**CAROLINA MOON
**HORNIN' IN
**SKIPPY
**LET'S COOL ONE
SUBURBAN EYES
**EVONCE

STRAIGHT NO CHASER
FOUR IN ONE
NICE WORK
MONK'S MOOD
WHO KNOWS
ASK ME NOW

*previously unissued on LP
**not previously issued on LP

'ROUND ABOUT MIDNIGHT, IN WALKED BUD, MONK'S MOOD, WHO KNOWS:
George Taitt, trumpet; Sahib Shihab, alto sax; Thelonious Monk, piano; Robert Paige, bass; Art Blakey, drums.

OFF MINOR, RUBY MY DEAR, APRIL IN PARIS, WELL YOU NEEDN'T, INTROSPECTION, NICE WORK:
Thelonious Monk, piano; Gene Ramey, bass; Art Blakey, drums.

I MEAN, YOU, EPISTROPHY, MISTERIOSO:
Milt Jackson, vibes; Thelonious Monk, piano; John Simmons, bass; Shadow Wilson, drums.

THELONIOUS, HUMPH, SUBURBAN EYES, EVONCE:
Idrees Sulieman, trumpet; Danny Quebec West, alto sax; Billy Smith, tenor sax; Thelonious Monk, piano; Gene Ramey, bass; Art Blakey, drums.

CAROLINA MOON, HORNIN' IN, SKIPPY, LET'S COOL ONE:
Kenny Dorham, trumpet; Lou Donaldson, alto sax; Lucky Thompson, tenor sax; Thelonious Monk, piano; Nelson Boyd, bass; Max Roach, drums.

STRAIGHT NO CHASER, FOUR IN ONE, ASK ME NOW:
Sahib Shihab, alto sax; Milt Jackson, vibes; Thelonious Monk, piano; Al McKibbon, bass; Art Blakey, drums.

THE DICTIONARY tells us that genius is exceptional natural capacity for creative and original conceptions and a genius is a person having such capacity. When considering the attributes of Thelonious Monk in the light of this definition, the title Genius Of Modern Music fits logically in all its aspects.

Monk's creativity is not limited to only the melodic or the harmonic or the rhythmic but embraces all three.

His harmonic innovations (new chord patterns and reinterpretations of older ones) were some of the most important germinating factors at Minton's. In fact Monk is synonymous with the Minton's of the earliest Forties because of the major role he played there in the birth of the new music.

The melodic side of Monk is exemplified best by his original compositions such as 'Round About Midnight, Well You Needn't, Ruby My Dear and Off Minor which have become permanent parts of the "Jazz library" through numerous in person performances and recordings by Monk and by people like Miles Davis, Bud Powell, Stan Getz and Jimmy Raney, George Wallington, Kenny Dorham and Barney Kessel.

Monk's rhythmic subtleties are more a permanent personal part of him than his melodic and harmonic contributions which have been assumed and interpreted by many other musicians. Among the pianists only Randy Weston has been directly influenced by him although Bud Powell and other pianists of that idiom exhibit Monkish flavor at various times. The rhythmic nuances by this master of time seem to escape Monk's detractors who give him little credit as a soloist but even if this side remains an enigma to them, the melodic and harmonic richness of performances like 'Round About Midnight, Ruby My Dear, April In Paris, Introspection, Ask Me Now and Four In One is proof enough of his singular prowess and certainly more than enough food for thought. The wit and warmth are in abundance.

His direct antecedents are hard to discern but there is a tacit link with the Harlem pianists of an earlier era. Occasionally this comes out into the open as in the striding left hand on Thelonious and the "train blues" on Well You Needn't, but it is the implied spirit which embodies more than one era of Jazz.

These two volumes represent the finest collection of Thelonious Monk to be found anywhere with lucid examples of his work from both the Forties and the Fifties.

Volume I [BLP 1510] contains recordings called from the mid and late Forties. There is the sombre beauty of the already immortalized 'Round About Midnight, the percussive, provocative minority of Off Minor, the sentiment without sentimentality of Ruby My Dear, the unflagging freshness of Well You Needn't, the Monk in Paris in April of

April in Paris, the questioning beauty of the heretofore unreleased Introspection, the humor and ingenuity of the one-noted Thelonious and the marvelous harmonic and rhythmic interplay between Milt Jackson and Monk on Epistrophy (written by Monk and Kenny Clarke). I Mean You (a theme borrowed by Gerry Mulligan for his Mood) and Misterioso.

Volume 2 [BLP 1511] has five tracks from the Forties. Suburban Eyes, written by tenorman Ike Quebec, and Evonce, a Quebec-Idrees Sulieman collaboration, feature Quebec's cousin Danny Quebec West on alto, the Dexter Gordonish (of that time) tenor of Billy Smith and the pungent trumpet of Idreess Sulieman in addition to Monk. Sulieman has only started to be appreciated recently. This group can be heard on Humph and Thelonious in Volume 1.

Two of the remaining Forties-recorded tracks are Monk's Mood, a piano solo integrated with the theme, as carried by George Taitt and Sahib Shihab, which expresses a melancholia with one cent worth of hope, and the up tempo Who Knows. These are done by the quintet which appears in 'Round About Midnight and In Walked Bud in Volume 1. Nice Work, a trio exploration of the Gershwin classic, stems from a 1947 trio session.

The majority of the tracks in Volume 2 were recorded in the Fifties. Four In One and Straight No Chaser reunite Monk with Milt Jackson, Sahib Shihab and Art Blakey. It is interesting and rewarding to hear the maturation of the four colleagues. Ask Me Now, done at the same session with just the trio, is worthy of the earlier great trio performances.

As composer-arranger for the sextet, Monk shows another facet of his skill. The 6/4 watts that he makes of Carolina Moon is an example of how to get away from the usual jazz beat and still swing. Lou Donaldson, Kenny Dorham and Lucky Thompson help considerably in the realization of this attempt (to say nothing of Max Roach) and make their solo power felt in the other numbers, Hornin' In, Skippy and Let's Cool One. Contrast these sextet tracks with the exact instrumentation of the Suburban Eyes group and you'll see where Monk has continued to grow while still remaining the individual personality who leads and influences modern music and its makers.

— IRA GITLER

Cover Design by REID K. MILES
Photo by FRANCIS WOLFF
Remastering by RUDY VAN GELDER

Users of Wide Range equipment should adjust their controls for RIAA curve.

GENIUS OF MODERN MUSIC VOLUME 2 1511
Artist THELONIOUS MONK

THE AMAZING BUD POWELL VOLUME 1 1503
Artist BUD POWELL
Cover Design by JOHN HERMANSADER
Cover Photo by FRANCIS WOLFF

THE AMAZING BUD POWELL VOLUME 2 1504
Artist BUD POWELL
Cover Design by JOHN HERMANSADER
Cover Photo by FRANCIS WOLFF

Opposite: GENIUS OF MODERN MUSIC VOLUME 2 1511 Artist THELONIOUS MONK Cover Design by REID MILES Cover Photo by FRANCIS WOLFF

volume two *blue note* **81511**

miles/wol*f*

THELO-
NIOUS
genius of modern music
MONK

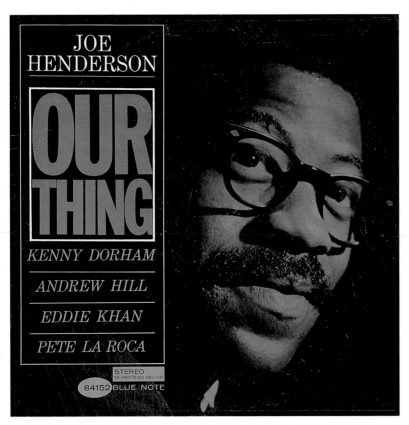

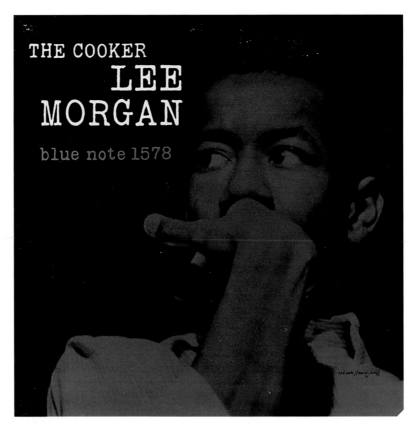

OUR THING 4152
Artist JOE HENDERSON
Cover Design by REID MILES
Cover Photo by FRANCIS WOLFF

THE COOKER 1578
Artist LEE MORGAN
Cover Design by REID MILES
Cover Photo by FRANCIS WOLFF

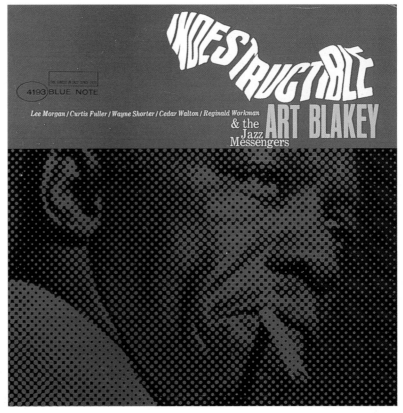

"BLUE SPIRITS" 4196
Artist FREDDIE HUBBARD
Cover Design by REID MILES
Cover Photo by REID MILES

INDESTRUCTIBLE 4193
Artist ART BLAKEY AND THE JAZZ MESSENGERS
Cover Design by REID MILES
Cover Photo by FRANCIS WOLFF

Opposite: WHISTLE STOP 4063 Artist KENNY DORHAM Cover Design by REID MILES Cover Photo by FRANCIS WOLFF

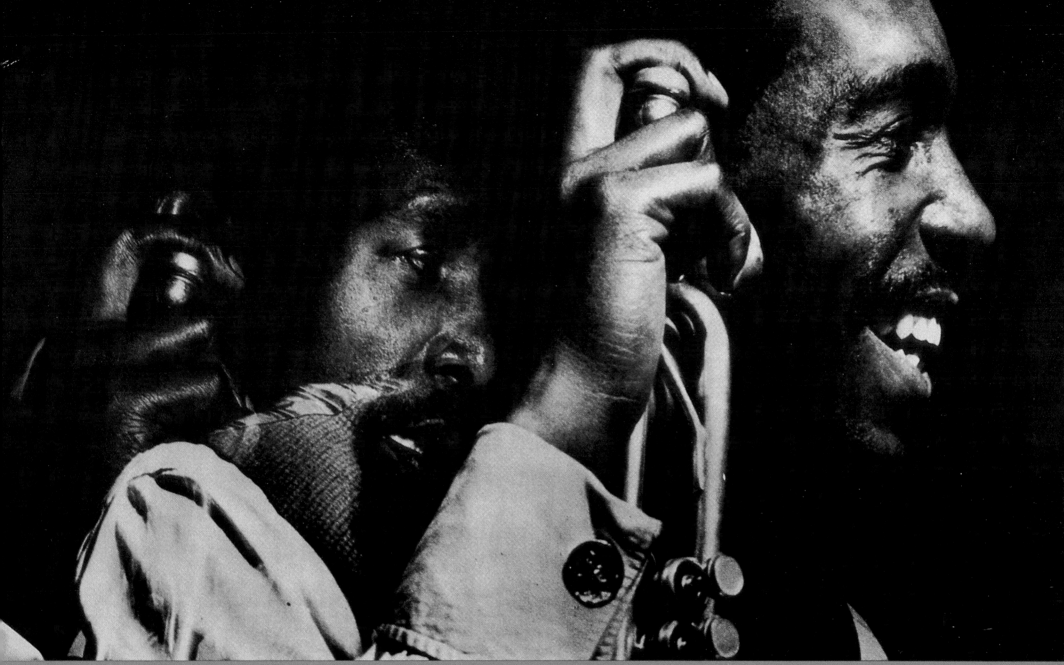

WHISTLE STOP

KENNY DORHAM   HANK MOBLEY
KENNY DREW   PAUL CHAMBERS
PHILLY JOE JONES

STEREO
THE FINEST IN JAZZ SINCE 1939

84063   BLUE NOTE

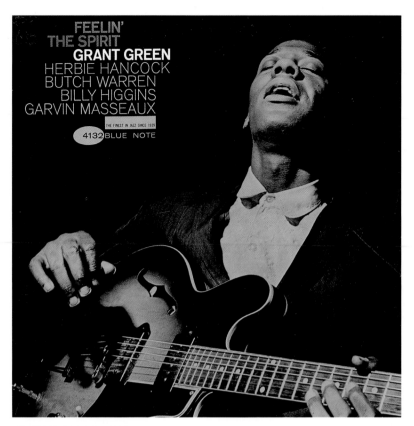

FEELIN' THE SPIRIT 4132
Artist GRANT GREEN
Cover Design by REID MILES
Cover Photo by FRANCIS WOLFF

"Frank tried to get the artist's real expression . . . the way he stood. Reid was more avant-garde and chic but the two together worked beautifully."
ALFRED LION

HANK MOBLEY QUINTET 1550
Artist HANK MOBLEY
Cover Design by HAROLD FEINSTEIN
Cover Photo by FRANCIS WOLFF

Opposite: A SWINGIN' AFFAIR 4133 · Artist DEXTER GORDON Cover Design by REID MILES Cover Photo by FRANCIS WOLFF

SHOUTIN'! 4145
Artist DON WILKERSON
Cover Design by REID MILES
Cover Photo by FRANCIS WOLFF

THE REAL McCOY 4264
Artist McCOY TYNER
Cover Design by REID MILES
Cover Photo by FRANCIS WOLFF

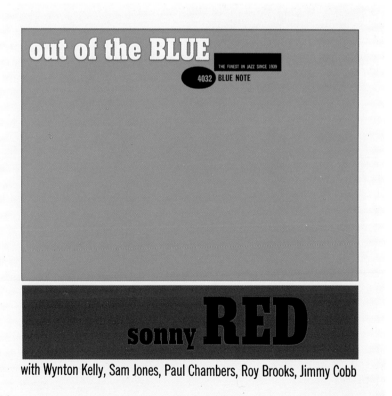

HEADIN' SOUTH 4062
Artist HORACE PARLAN
Cover Design by RONNIE BRATHWAITE

OUT OF THE BLUE 4032
Artist SONNY RED
Cover Design by REID MILES
Cover Photo by FRANCIS WOLFF

Opposite: NEWK'S TIME 4001 Artist SONNY ROLLINS Cover Photo by FRANCIS WOLFF

stereo

BST 84001

BLP 4001

NEWK'S TIME

SONNY ROLLINS

THE FINEST IN JAZZ SINCE 1939

BLUE NOTE

A PRODUCT OF LIBERTY RECORDS

SEARCH FOR THE NEW LAND 4169
Artist LEE MORGAN
Cover Design by REID MILES
Cover Photo by FRANCIS WOLFF

THE TIME IS RIGHT 4025
Artist LOU DONALDSON
Cover Design by REID MILES
Cover Photo by FRANCIS WOLFF

CONTOURS 4206
Artist SAM RIVERS
Cover Design by REID MILES
Cover Photo by REID MILES

HUSTLIN' 4162
Artist STANLEY TURRENTINE
Cover Design by REID MILES
Cover Photo by REID MILES

Opposite: MY POINT OF VIEW 4126 Artist HERBIE HANCOCK Cover Design by REID MILES Cover Photo by REID MILES

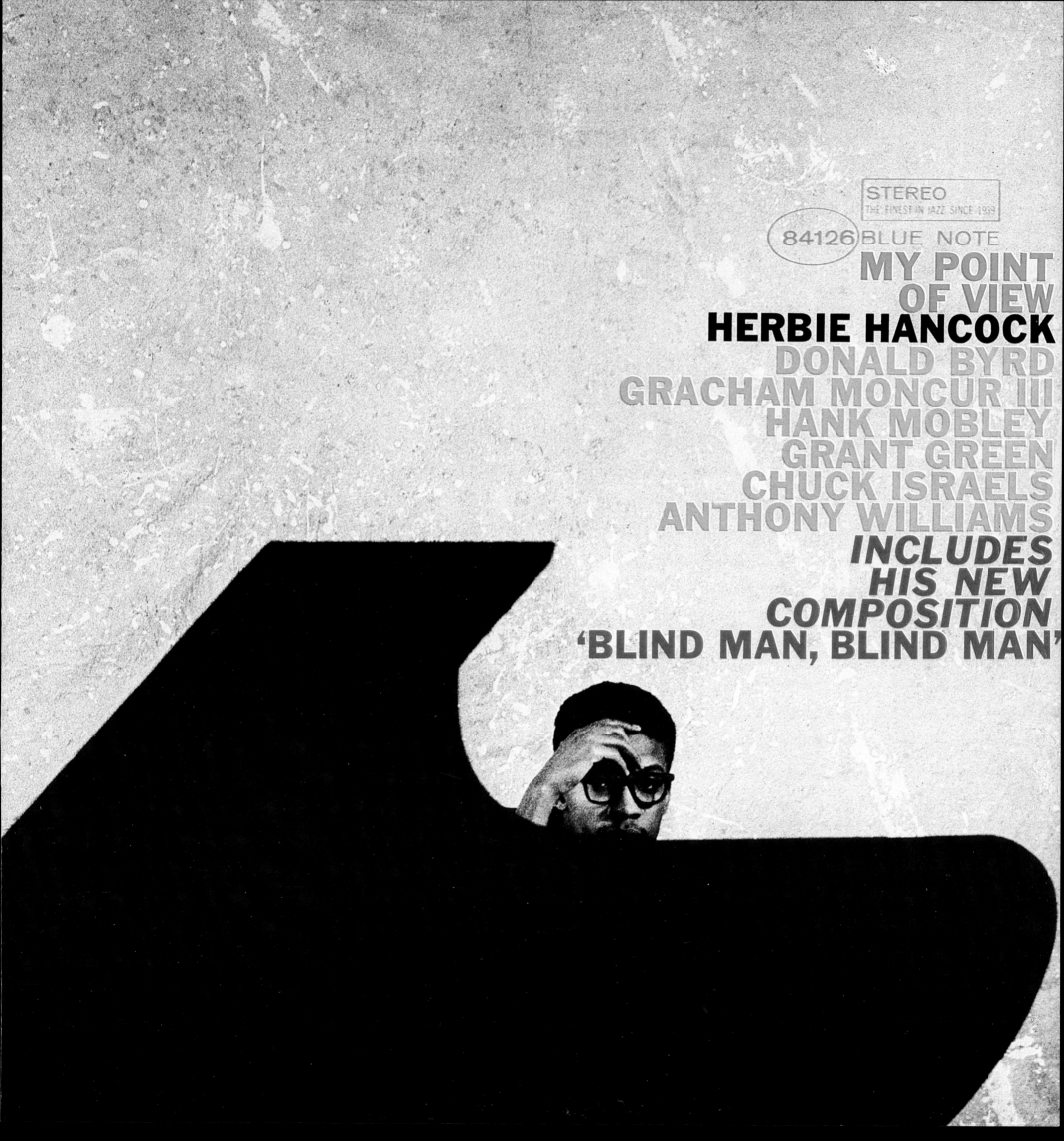

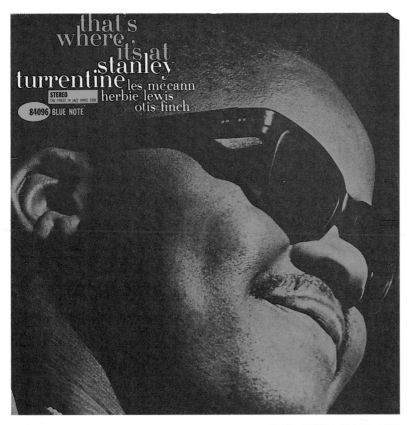

THAT'S WHERE IT'S AT 4096
Artist STANLEY TURRENTINE
Cover Design by REID MILES
Cover Photo by FRANCIS WOLFF

THE FREEDOM RIDER 4156
Artist ART BLAKEY AND THE JAZZ MESSENGERS
Cover Design by REID MILES
Cover Photo by FRANCIS WOLFF

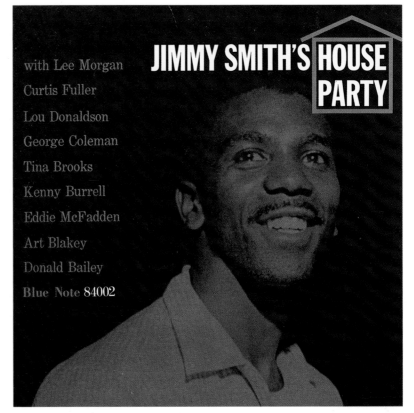

MOANIN' 4003
Artist ART BLAKEY AND THE JAZZ MESSENGERS
Cover Photo by BUCK HOEFFLER

HOUSE PARTY 4002
Artist JIMMY SMITH
Cover Photo by FRANCIS WOLFF

Opposite: ALONG CAME JOHN 4130 Artist JOHN PATTON Cover Design by REID MILES Cover Photo by FRANCIS WOLFF

ALONG CAME JOHN

JOHN PATTON

ORGAN

THE FINEST IN JAZZ SINCE 1939

4130 BLUE NOTE

FRED JACKSON/TENOR SAX
HAROLD VICK/TENOR SAX
GRANT GREEN/GUITAR
BEN DIXON/DRUMS

THE SIDEWINDER 4157
Artist LEE MORGAN
Cover Design by REID MILES
Cover Photo by FRANCIS WOLFF

"Frank always hated it when I cropped one of his photographs of his artists through the forehead."
REID MILES

UNDERCURRENT 4059
Artist KENNY DREW
Cover Design by REID MILES
Cover Photo by FRANCIS WOLFF

Opposite: TRUE BLUE 4041 Artist TINA BROOKS Cover Design by REID MILES Cover Photo by FRANCIS WOLFF

Freddie Hubbard, Duke Jordan, Sam Jones, Art Taylor

84041) BLUE NOTE TRUE BLUE TINA BROOKS

Blue In and Out

Gabrial Blue

Alice Blue

Blue-Hoo

Sticks like Blue

Blue Away

True Blue

Too Blue

I Love Blue

Blue or False

Blue Jeans

Blue Note

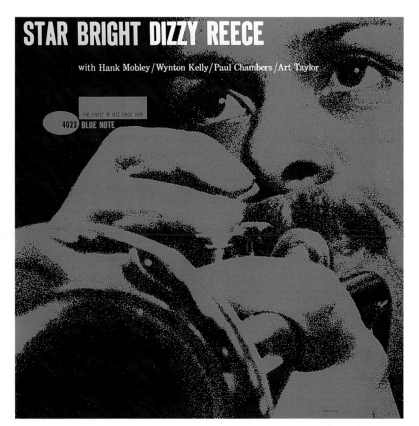

STAR BRIGHT 4023
Artist DIZZY REECE
Cover Design by REID MILES
Cover Photo by FRANCIS WOLFF

A FICKLE SONANCE 4089
Artist JACKIE McLEAN
Cover Design by REID MILES
Cover Photo by FRANCIS WOLFF

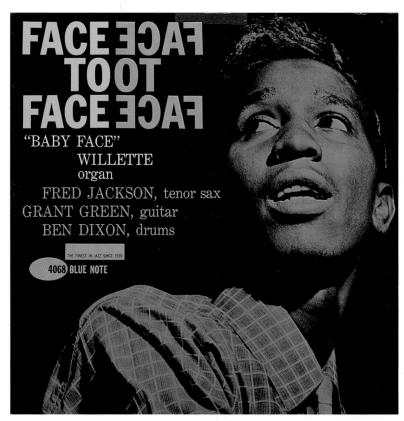

FACE TO FACE 4068
Artist BABY FACE WILLETTE
Cover Design by REID MILES
Cover Photo by FRANCIS WOLFF

INTRODUCING JOHNNY GRIFFIN 1533
Artist JOHNNY GRIFFIN
Cover Design by REID MILES
Cover Photo by FRANCIS WOLFF

Opposite: IDLE MOMENTS 4154 Artist GRANT GREEN Cover Design by REID MILES Cover Photo by FRANCIS WOLFF

STEREO
THE FINEST IN JAZZ SINCE 1939
84154 BLUE NOTE

DLE MOMENTS GRANT GREEN

E HENDERSON/BOBBY HUTCHERSON/DUKE PEARSON/BOB CRANSHAW/AL HAREWOOD

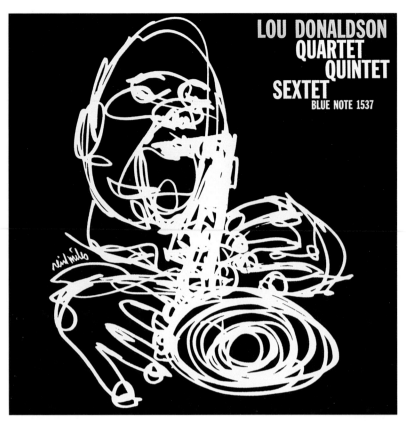

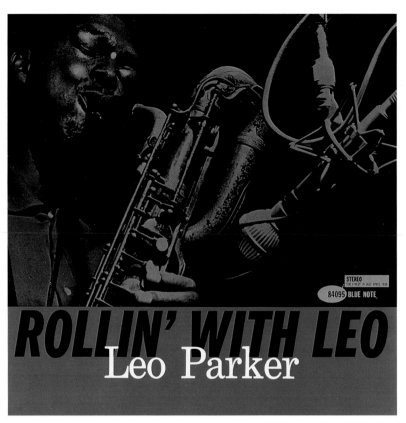

QUARTET/QUINTET/SEXTET 1537
Artist LOU DONALDSON
Cover Design by REID MILES
Cover Photo by FRANCIS WOLFF

ROLLIN' WITH LEO 4095
Artist LEO PARKER
Cover Design by REID MILES
Cover Photo by FRANCIS WOLFF

ADAM'S APPLE 4232
Artist WAYNE SHORTER
Cover Design by REID MILES
Cover Photo by FRANCIS WOLFF

HANK MOBLEY SEXTET 1540
Artist HANK MOBLEY
Cover Design by REID MILES
Cover Photo by FRANCIS WOLFF

Opposite: ROUGH 'N TUMBLE 4240 Artist STANLEY TURRENTINE Cover Design by GEORGE WRIGHT Cover Photo by FRANCIS WOLFF

ROUGH 'N TUMBLE

STANLEY TURRENTINE

BLUE MITCHELL
JAMES SPAULDING
PEPPER ADAMS
GRANT GREEN
McCOY TYNER
BOB CRANSHAW
MICKEY ROKER

THE FINEST IN JAZZ SINCE 1939
BLUE NOTE
A PRODUCT OF LIBERTY RECORDS

BLP 4240

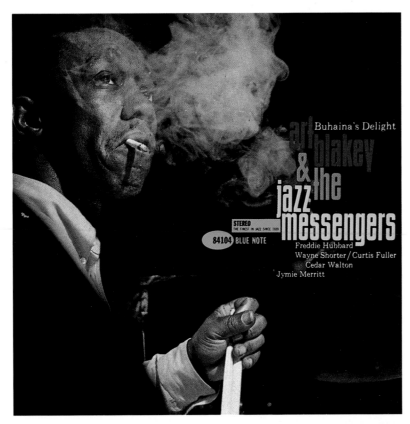

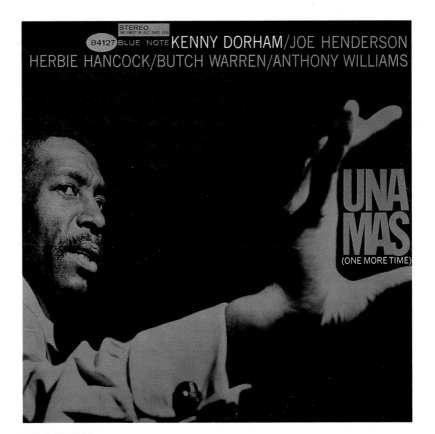

BUHAINA'S DELIGHT 4104
Artist ART BLAKEY AND THE JAZZ MESSENGERS
Cover Design by REID MILES
Cover Photo by FRANCIS WOLFF

UNA MAS 4127
Artist KENNY DORHAM
Cover Design by REID MILES
Cover Photo by FRANCIS WOLFF

BLUE & SENTIMENTAL 4098
Artist IKE QUEBEC
Cover Design by REID MILES
Cover Photo by FRANCIS WOLFF

LEE MORGAN 1541
Artist LEE MORGAN
Cover Design by REID MILES
Cover Photo by FRANCIS WOLFF

Opposite: SOUL STATION 4031 Artist HANK MOBLEY Cover Design by REID MILES Cover Photo by FRANCIS WOLFF

SOUL STATION HANK MOBLEY
WITH ART BLAKEY
WYNTON KELLY, PAUL CHAMBERS

STEREO
THE FINEST IN JAZZ SINCE 1939
84031 BLUE NOTE

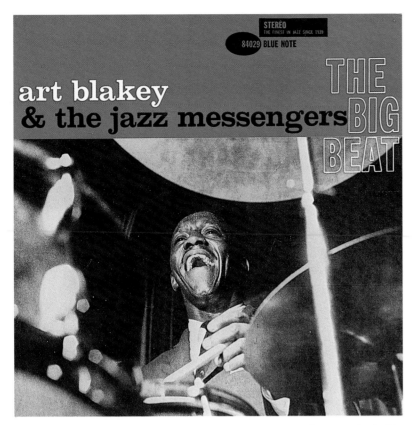

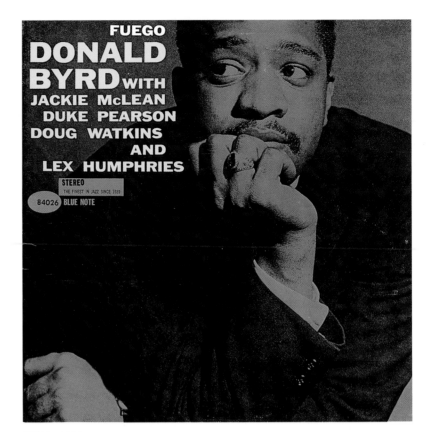

THE BIG BEAT 4029
Artist ART BLAKEY AND THE JAZZ MESSENGERS
Cover Design by REID MILES
Cover Photo by FRANCIS WOLFF

FUEGO 4026
Artist DONALD BYRD
Cover Design by REID MILES
Cover Photo by FRANCIS WOLFF

BLOWING IN FROM CHICAGO 1549
Artist CLIFF JORDAN/JOHN GILMORE
Cover Design by HAROLD FEINSTEIN
Cover Photo by FRANCIS WOLFF

'GOOD MOVE!' 4158
Artist FREDDIE ROACH
Cover Design by REID MILES
Cover Photo by FRANCIS WOLFF

Opposite: SONNY ROLLINS VOLUME 2 1558 Artist SONNY ROLLINS Cover Design by HAROLD FEINSTEIN Cover Photo by FRANCIS WOLFF

stereo

BST 81558

BLP 1558

THE FINEST IN JAZZ SINCE 1939

BLUE NOTE

A PRODUCT OF LIBERTY RECORDS

Vol. 2

SONNY ROLLINS

Jay Jay Johnson
Horace Silver
Thelonious Monk
Paul Chambers
Art Blakey

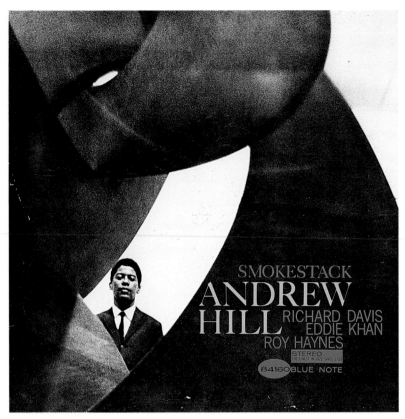

SMOKESTACK 4160
Artist ANDREW HILL
Cover Design by REID MILES
Cover Photo by REID MILES

"Gosh this is different! . . . that's Blue Note . . .

that's what we want . . ."

ALFRED LION

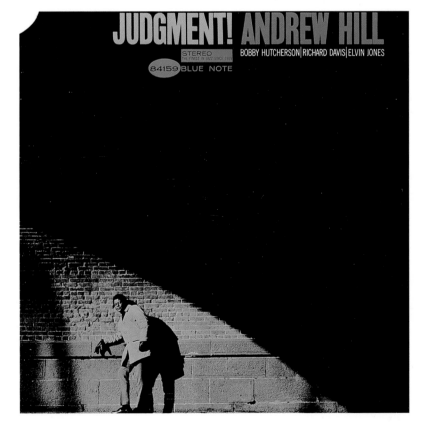

JUDGMENT! 4159
Artist ANDREW HILL
Cover Design by REID MILES
Cover Photo by FRANCIS WOLFF

Opposite: 'OUT TO LUNCH!' 4163 Artist ERIC DOLPHY Cover Design by REID MILES Cover Photo by REID MILES

ONE FLIGHT UP 4176
Artist DEXTER GORDON
Cover Design by REID MILES
Cover Photo by FRANCIS WOLFF

GETTIN' AROUND 4204
Artist DEXTER GORDON
Cover Design by REID MILES
Cover Photo by FRANCIS WOLFF

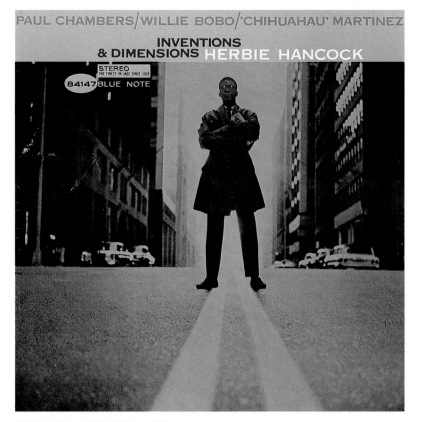

LET ME TELL YOU 'BOUT IT 4087
Artist LEO PARKER
Cover Photo by FRANCIS WOLFF

INVENTIONS & DIMENSIONS 4147
Artist HERBIE HANCOCK
Cover Design by REID MILES
Cover Photo by FRANCIS WOLFF

Opposite: HOME COOKIN' 4050 Artist JIMMY SMITH Cover Design by REID MILES Cover Photo by FRANCIS WOLFF

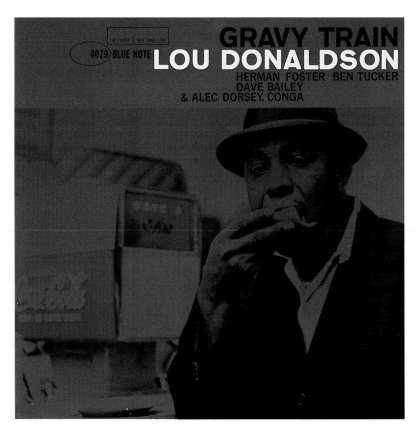

'JUJU' 4182
Artist WAYNE SHORTER
Cover Design by REID MILES
Cover Photo by REID MILES

GRAVY TRAIN 4079
Artist LOU DONALDSON
Cover Design by REID MILES
Cover Photo by RONNIE BRATHWAITE

MO' GREENS PLEASE 4128
Artist FREDDIE ROACH
Cover Design by REID MILES
Cover Photo by RONNIE BRATHWAITE

ONE STEP BEYOND 4137
Artist JACKIE McLEAN
Cover Design by REID MILES
Cover Photo by FRANCIS WOLFF

Opposite: INTO SOMETHIN' 4187 Artist LARRY YOUNG Cover Design by REID MILES Cover Photo by FRANCIS WOLFF

into somethin!
larry young

Sam Rivers
Grant Green
Elvin Jones

STEREO
THE FINEST IN JAZZ SINCE 1939
84187 BLUE NOTE

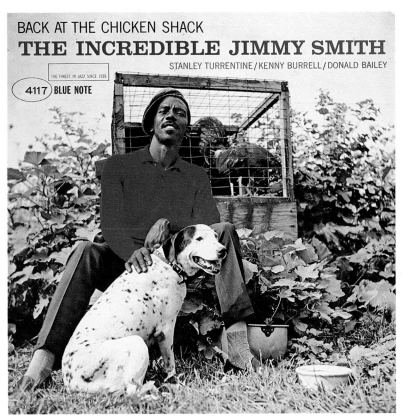

BACK AT THE CHICKEN SHACK 4117
Artist JIMMY SMITH
Cover Design by REID MILES
Cover Photo by FRANCIS WOLFF

SONG FOR MY FATHER 4185
Artist HORACE SILVER
Cover Design by REID MILES
Cover Photo by FRANCIS WOLFF

FINGER POPPIN' 4008
Artist HORACE SILVER
Cover Design by REID MILES
Cover Photo by FRANCIS WOLFF

OPEN SESAME 4040
Artist FREDDIE HUBBARD
Cover Design by REID MILES
Cover Photo by FRANCIS WOLFF

Opposite: DEXTER CALLING . . . 4083 Artist DEXTER GORDON Cover Photo by FRANCIS WOLFF

UP & DOWN 4082
Artist HORACE PARLAN
Cover Design by REID MILES
Cover Photo by FRANCIS WOLFF

"It didn't mean you had to have full colour —
two colours didn't hurt that product at all. The few
full colour covers I did were not as
strong as the ones with black and white and red."
REID MILES

NO ROOM FOR SQUARES 4149
Artist HANK MOBLEY
Cover Design by REID MILES
Cover Photo by FRANCIS WOLFF

Opposite: SUNNY SIDE UP 4036 Artist LOU DONALDSON Cover Design by REID MILES

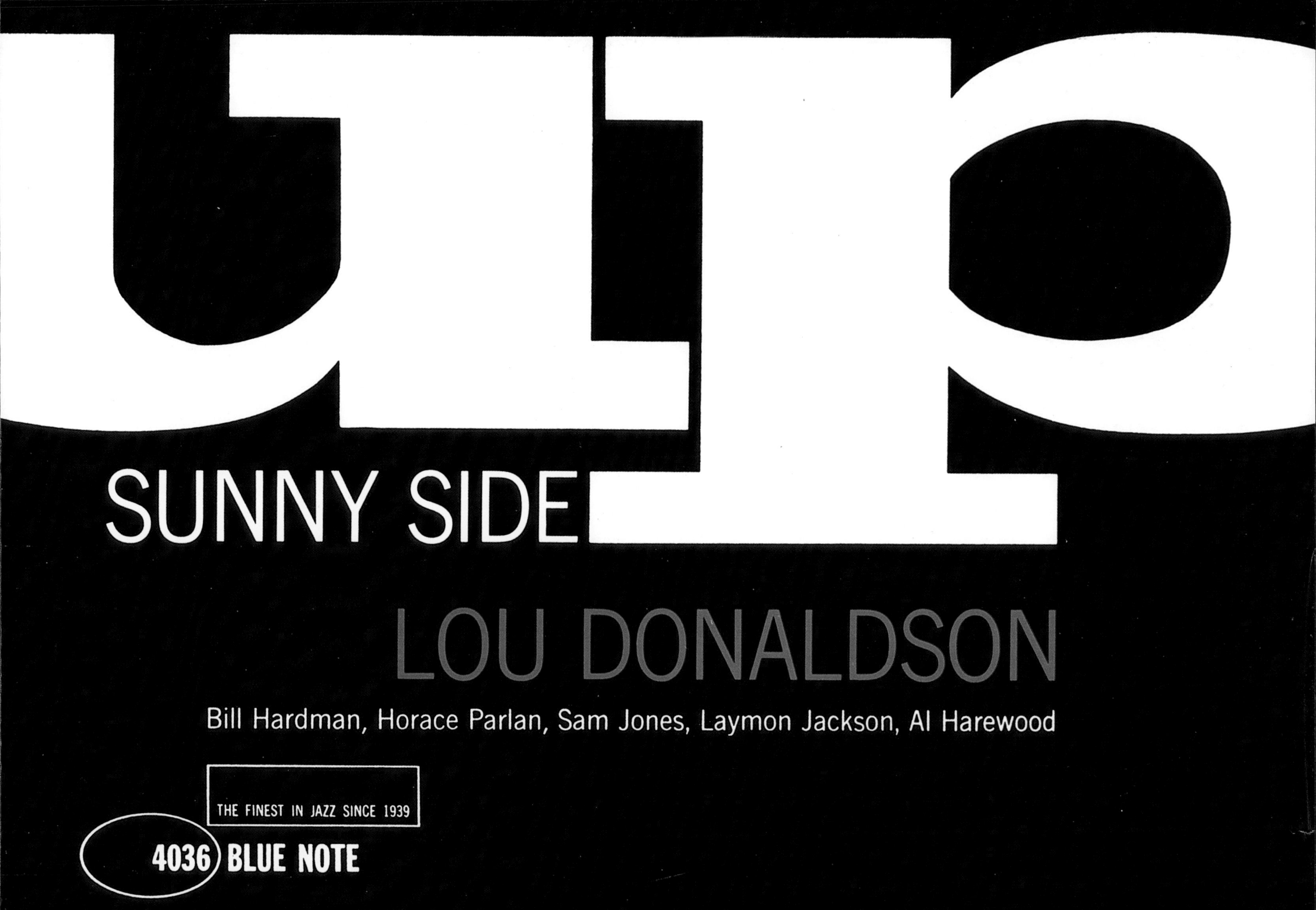

up

SUNNY SIDE

LOU DONALDSON

Bill Hardman, Horace Parlan, Sam Jones, Laymon Jackson, Al Harewood

THE FINEST IN JAZZ SINCE 1939

4036 **BLUE NOTE**

BLUES WALK 1593
Artist LOU DONALDSON
Cover Photo by FRANCIS WOLFF

THE MAGNIFICENT THAD JONES 1527
Artist THAD JONES
Cover Photo by FRANCIS WOLFF

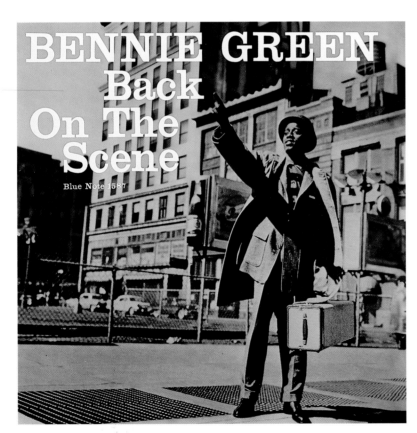

BACK ON THE SCENE 1587
Artist BENNIE GREEN
Cover Photo by FRANCIS WOLFF

WHIMS OF CHAMBERS 1534
Artist PAUL CHAMBERS
Cover Design by REID MILES
Cover Photo by FRANCIS WOLFF

Opposite: AT THE "GOLDEN CIRCLE" VOLUME 1 4224 Artist ORNETTE COLEMAN Cover Design by REID MILES Cover Photo by FRANCIS WOLFF

IT MIGHT AS WELL BE SPRING 4105
Artist IKE QUEBEC
Cover Design by REID MILES
Cover Photo by FRANCIS WOLFF

6 PIECES OF SILVER 1539
Artist HORACE SILVER
Cover Design by REID MILES
Cover Photo by FRANCIS WOLFF

STEPPIN' OUT! 4138
Artist HAROLD VICK
Cover Design by REID MILES
Cover Photo by REID MILES

PAGE ONE 4140
Artist JOE HENDERSON
Cover Design by REID MILES
Cover Photo by FRANCIS WOLFF

Opposite: MIDNIGHT SPECIAL 4078 Artist JIMMY SMITH Cover Photo by FRANCIS WOLFF

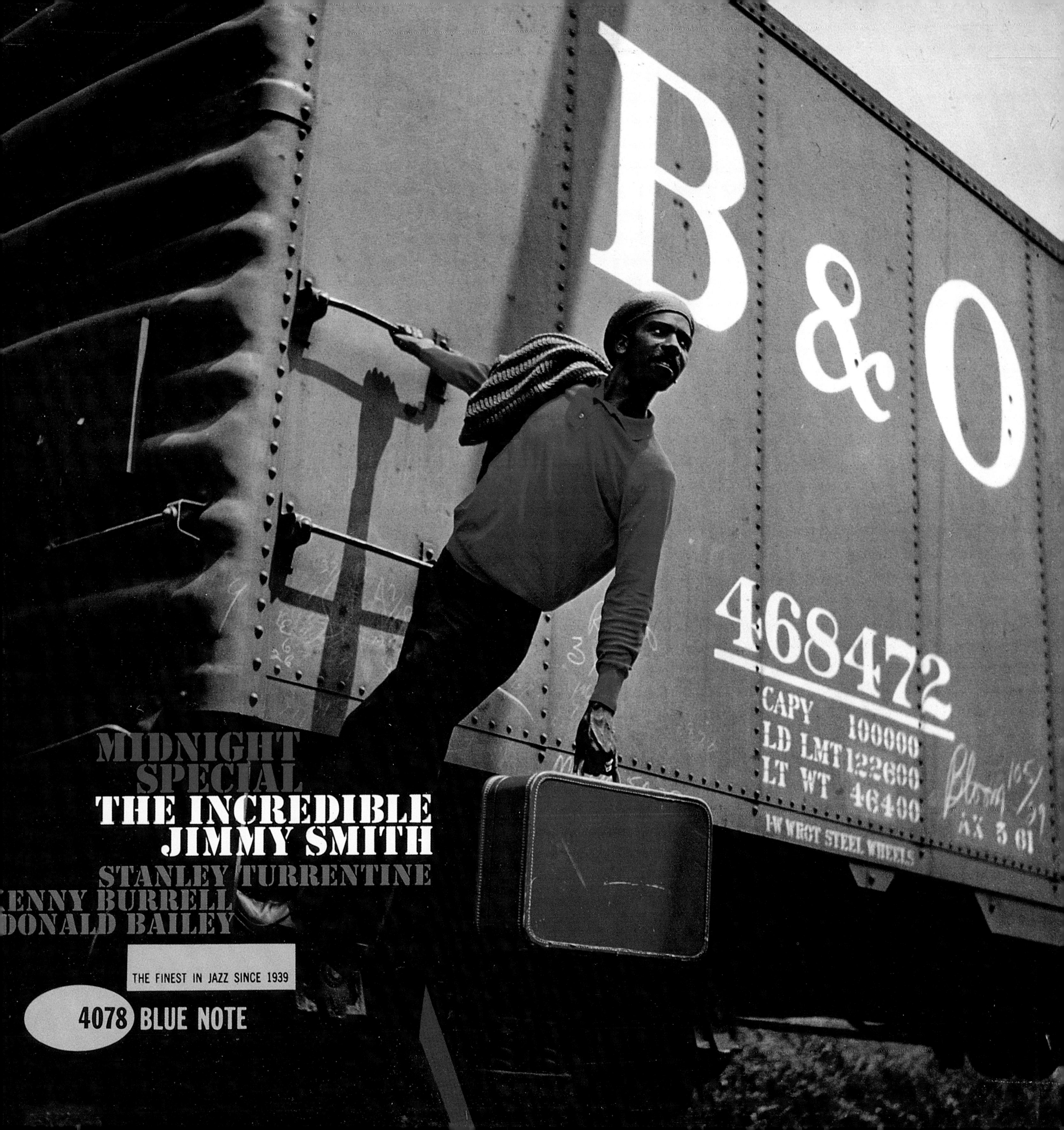
B&O
468472
CAPY 100000
LD LMT 122600
LT WT 46400
MIDNIGHT
SPECIAL
THE INCREDIBLE
JIMMY SMITH
STANLEY TURRENTINE
KENNY BURRELL
DONALD BAILEY
THE FINEST IN JAZZ SINCE 1939
4078 BLUE NOTE

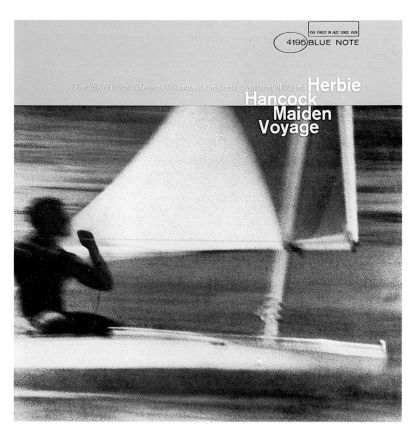

MAIDEN VOYAGE 4195
Artist HERBIE HANCOCK
Cover Design by REID MILES
Cover Photo by REID MILES

"WAHOO!" 4191
Artist DUKE PEARSON
Cover Design by REID MILES
Cover Photo by REID MILES

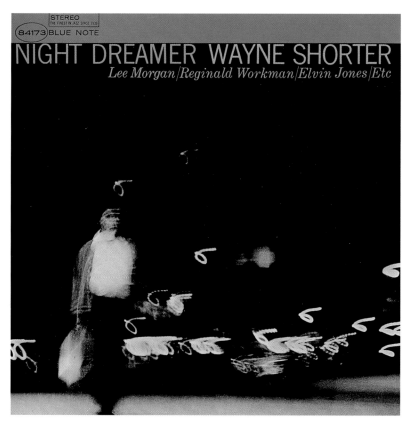

FREEFORM 4118
Artist DONALD BYRD
Cover Design by REID MILES
Cover Photo by REID MILES

NIGHT DREAMER 4173
Artist WAYNE SHORTER
Cover Design by REID MILES
Cover Photo by FRANCIS WOLFF

Opposite: LIKE SOMEONE IN LOVE 4245 Artist ART BLAKEY AND THE JAZZ MESSENGERS Cover Design by REID MILES Cover Photo by REID MILES

BLP 4245

THE FINEST IN JAZZ SINCE 1939

BLUE NOTE
A PRODUCT OF LIBERTY RECORDS

ART BLAKEY AND THE JAZZ MESSENGERS

LEE MORGAN/WAYNE SHORTER/BOBBY TIMMONS/JYMIE MERRITT

LIKESOMEONEINLOVE

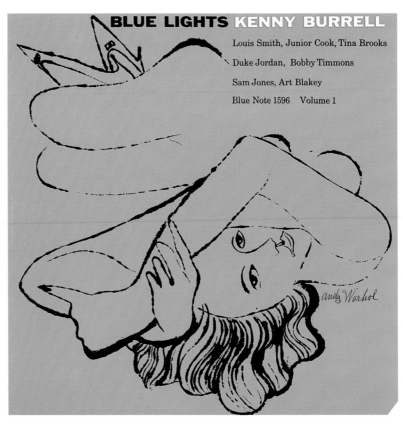

BLUE LIGHTS VOLUME 1 1596
Artist KENNY BURRELL
Cover Design by REID MILES & ANDY WARHOL

"That Blue Note era would never have
happened in the context of a large company . . .
it was a personalized, individual, approach."
RUDY VAN GELDER

60

BLUE LIGHTS VOLUME 2 1597
Artist KENNY BURRELL
Cover Design by REID MILES & ANDY WARHOL

Opposite: THE CONGREGATION 1580 Artist JOHNNY GRIFFIN Cover Design by REID MILES & ANDY WARHOL

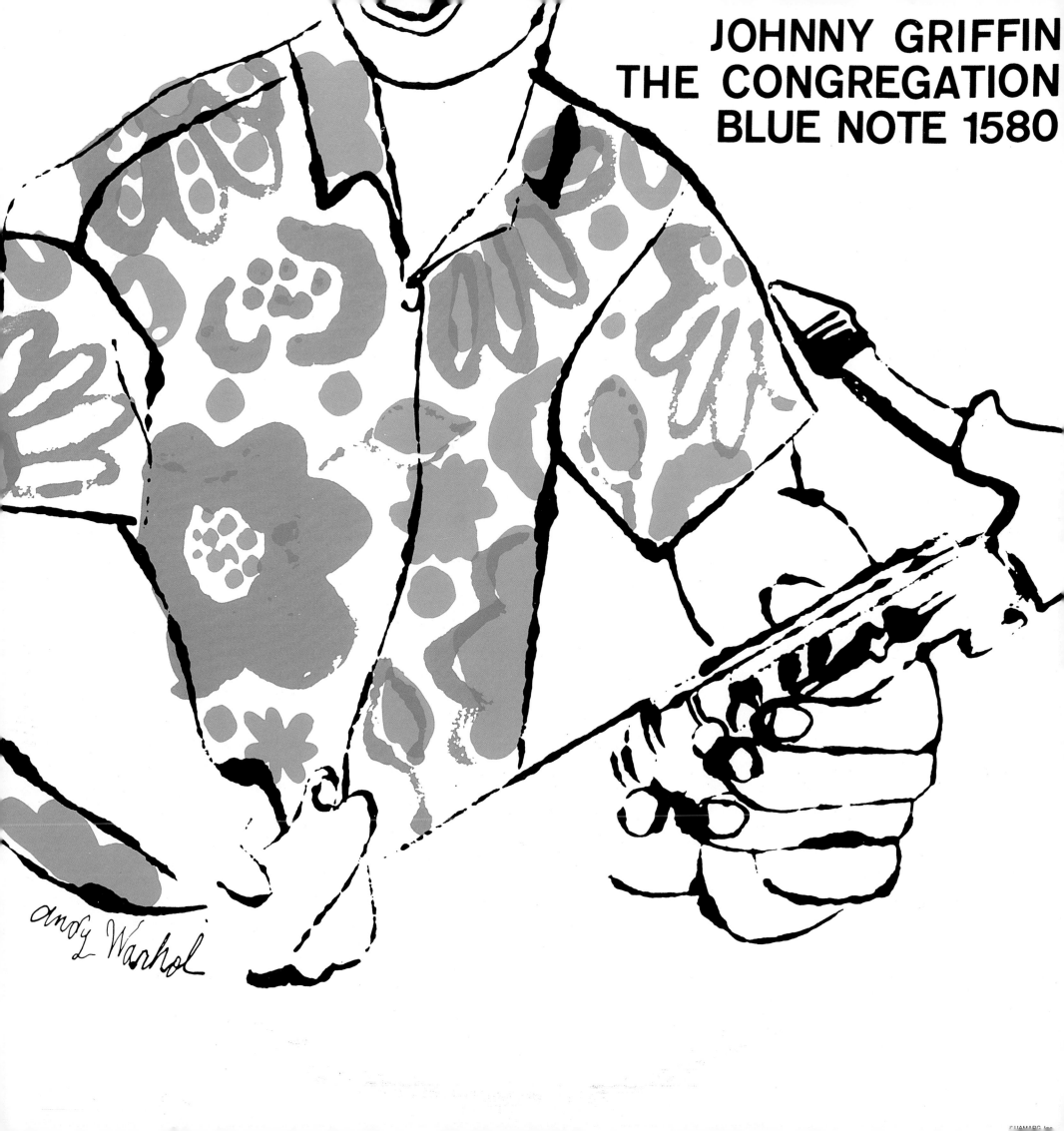

JOHNNY GRIFFIN
THE CONGREGATION
BLUE NOTE 1580

Andy Warhol

OH BABY! 4192
Artist JOHN PATTON
Cover Design by RONNIE BRATHWAITE

"BROWN SUGAR" 4168
Artist FREDDIE ROACH
Cover Design by REID MILES
Cover Photo by RONNIE BRATHWAITE

DOWN WITH IT! 4214
Artist BLUE MITCHELL
Cover Design by REID MILES
Cover Photo by REID MILES

I WANT TO HOLD YOUR HAND 4202
Artist GRANT GREEN
Cover Design by REID MILES
Cover Photo by REID MILES

Opposite: THE NATURAL SOUL 4108 Artist LOU DONALDSON Cover Design by REID MILES

STEREO
THE FINEST IN JAZZ SINCE 1939
84108 BLUE NOTE®

the natural soul

lou donaldson

tommy turrentine

grant green

john patton

ben dixon

THE TOKYO BLUES 4110
Artist HORACE SILVER
Cover Design by REID MILES
Cover Photo by FRANCIS WOLFF

THE CAPE VERDEAN BLUES 4220
Artist HORACE SILVER
Cover Design by REID MILES
Cover Photo by REID MILES

"GOOD GRACIOUS!" 4125
Artist LOU DONALDSON
Cover Design by REID MILES
Cover Photo by RONNIE BRATHWAITE

LET 'EM ROLL 4239
Artist JOHN PATTON
Cover Design by REID MILES

Opposite: COOL STRUTTIN' 1588 Artist SONNY CLARK

STEREO · BST 84238 · BLP 4238 · BLUE NOTE

HAPPENINGS
BOBBY HUTCHERSON
HERBIE HANCOCK/BOB CRANSHAW/JOE CHAMBERS

DONALD BYRD
Sonny Red/Hank Mobley/McCoy Tyner/Walter Booker/Freddie Waits
"MUSTANG!"

HAPPENINGS 4231
Artist BOBBY HUTCHERSON
Cover Design by REID MILES
Cover Photo by REID MILES

"MUSTANG!" 4238
Artist DONALD BYRD
Cover Design by REID MILES
Cover Photo by REID MILES

"A NEW CONCEPTION"
WHEN I FALL IN LOVE
I'LL NEVER SMILE AGAIN
DETOUR AHEAD SAM
THAT'S ALL RIVERS
WHAT A DIFFERENCE A DAY MAKES
TEMPTATION
SECRET LOVE

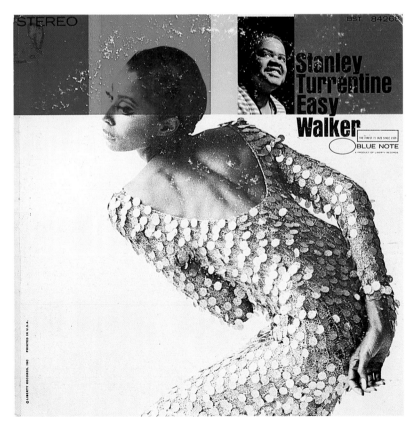

STEREO · BST 84268 · Stanley Turrentine Easy Walker · BLUE NOTE

"A NEW CONCEPTION" 4249
Artist SAM RIVERS
Cover Design by REID MILES
Cover Photo by REID MILES

EASY WALKER 4268
Artist STANLEY TURRENTINE
Cover Design by REID MILES
Cover Photo by FRANCIS WOLFF

Opposite: ALLIGATOR BOGALOO 4263 Artist LOU DONALDSON Cover Design by REID MILES Cover Photo by REID MILES

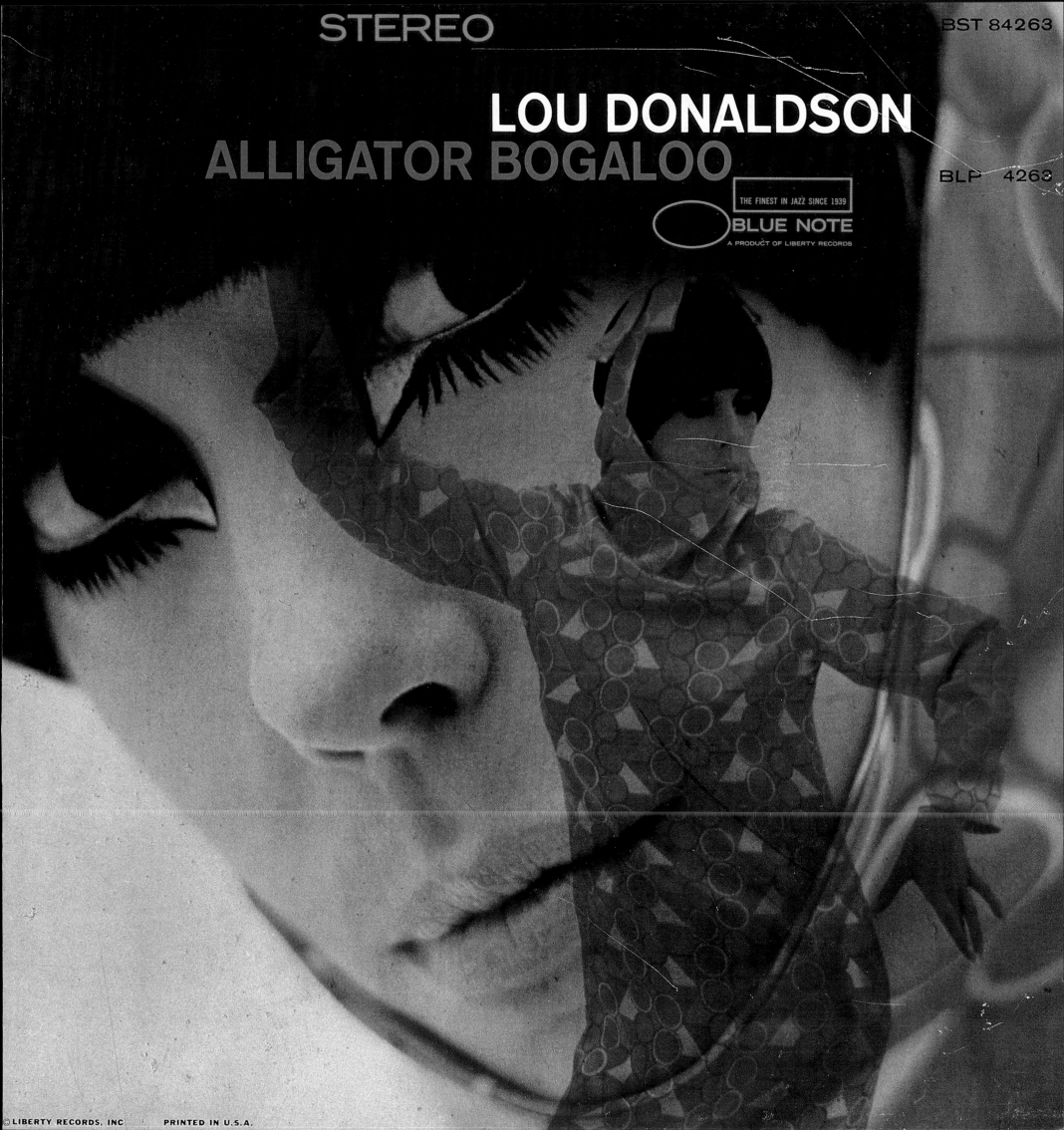

BOSSA NOVA SOUL SAMBA 4114
Artist IKE QUEBEC
Cover Design by REID MILES
Cover Photo by REID MILES

"Those covers look as fresh today as they did
twenty years ago . . ."
ALFRED LION

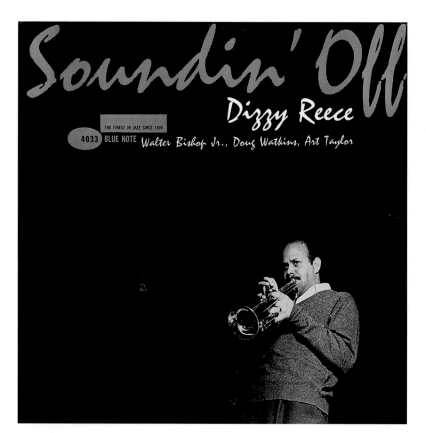

SOUNDIN' OFF 4033
Artist DIZZY REECE
Cover Design by REID MILES
Cover Photo by FRANCIS WOLFF

Opposite: AFRO-CUBAN 1535 Artist KENNY DORHAM Cover Design by REID MILES Cover Photo by FRANCIS WOLFF

AFRO-CUBAN
KENNY DORHAM

BLUE NOTE
1535

HUB CAP/FREDDIE HUBBARD

julian priester/jimmy heath/cedar walton/larry ridley/philly joe jones

84073 BLUE NOTE.
THE FINEST IN JAZZ SINCE 1939

MILT JACKSON

with john lewis, percy heath, kenny clarke, lou donaldson
and the THELONIOUS MONK QUINTET blue note 1509

miles/wolf

HUB CAP 4073
Artist FREDDIE HUBBARD
Cover Design by REID MILES
Cover Photo by FRANCIS WOLFF

MILT JACKSON 1509
Artist MILT JACKSON
Cover Design by REID MILES
Cover Photo by FRANCIS WOLFF

70

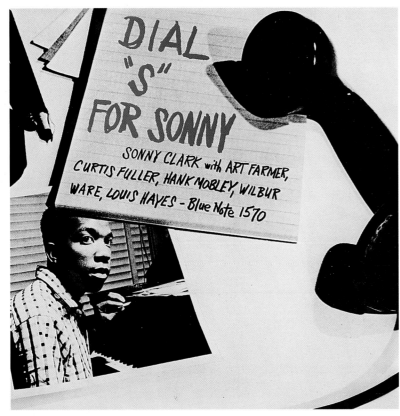

DIAL "S" FOR SONNY

SONNY CLARK with ART FARMER, CURTIS FULLER, HANK MOBLEY, WILBUR WARE, LOUIS HAYES - Blue Note 1570

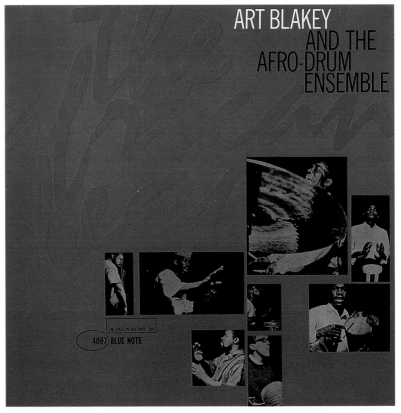

ART BLAKEY AND THE AFRO-DRUM ENSEMBLE

4097 BLUE NOTE
THE FINEST IN JAZZ SINCE 1939

DIAL "S" FOR SONNY 1570
Artist SONNY CLARK
Cover Design by REID MILES
Cover Photo by WILLIAM CONNORS

THE AFRICAN BEAT 4097
Artist ART BLAKEY AND THE AFRO-DRUM ENSEMBLE
Cover Design by REID MILES
Cover Photo by FRANCIS WOLFF

Opposite: BLUESNIK 4067 Artist JACKIE McLEAN Cover Design by REID MILES Cover Photo by FRANCIS WOLFF

BLUESNIK

JACKIE McLEAN

FREDDIE HUBBARD, KENNY DREW, DOUG WATKINS
AND PETE LA ROCA

STEREO
THE FINEST IN JAZZ SINCE 1939

84067 BLUE NOTE

COMPONENTS 4213
Artist BOBBY HUTCHERSON
Cover Design by REID MILES
Cover Photo by REID MILES

"Fifty bucks an album . . . they loved it, thought it was modern, they thought it went with the music . . . one or two colours to work with at that time and some outrageous graphics!"
REID MILES

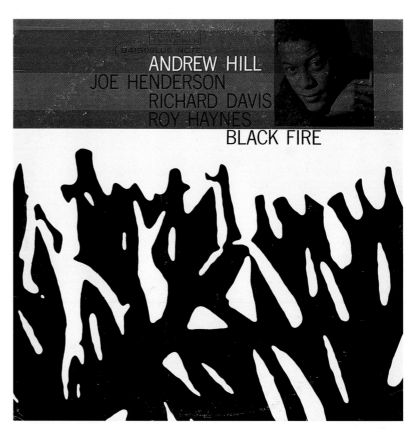

BLACK FIRE 4151
Artist ANDREW HILL
Cover Design by REID MILES
Cover Photo by FRANCIS WOLFF

Opposite: EVOLUTION 4153 Artist GRACHAN MONCUR III Cover Design by REID MILES Cover Photo by FRANCIS WOLFF

TWO SOULS IN ONE 4148
Artist GEORGE BRAITH
Cover Design by REID MILES
Cover Photo by FRANCIS WOLFF

LEE MORGAN INDEED! 1538
Artist LEE MORGAN
Cover Design by REID MILES
Cover Photo by FRANCIS WOLFF

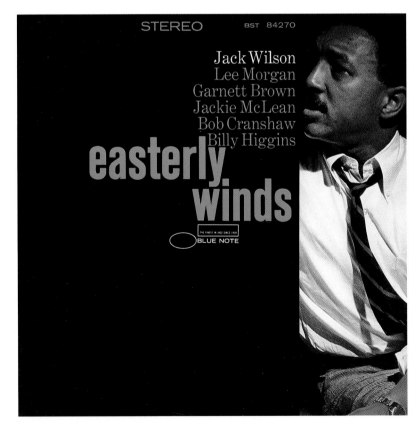

ACTION 4218
Artist JACKIE McLEAN
Cover Design by REID MILES
Cover Photo by FRANCIS WOLFF

EASTERLY WINDS 4270
Artist JACK WILSON
Cover Design by REID MILES
Cover Photo by FRANCIS WOLFF

Opposite: BASRA 4205 Artist PETE LA ROCA Cover Design by REID MILES Cover Photo by FRANCIS WOLFF

BASRA

JOE HENDERSON STEVE KUHN STEVE SWALLOW

PETE LA ROCA

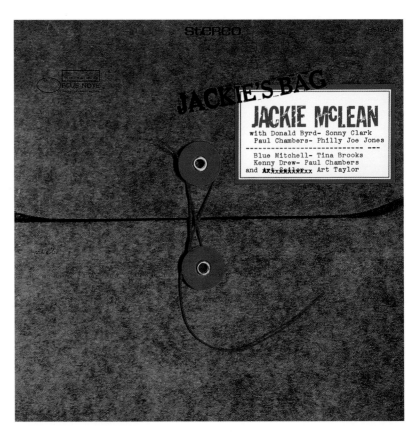

PECKIN' TIME 1574
Artist HANK MOBLEY

"Jackie's Bag, Frank hated that . . . there was no photograph!"
REID MILES

JACKIE'S BAG 4051
Artist JACKIE McLEAN
Cover Design by REID MILES

Opposite: SPRING 4216 Artist ANTHONY WILLIAMS Cover Design by REID MILES

4216 BLUE NOTE

THE FINEST IN JAZZ SINCE 1939

spring/anthony williams

"Speak No Evil"

STEREO
THE FINEST IN JAZZ SINCE 1939
84194 BLUE NOTE

WAYNE SHORTER
*Freddie Hubbard / Herbie Hancock / Ron Carter
Elvin Jones*

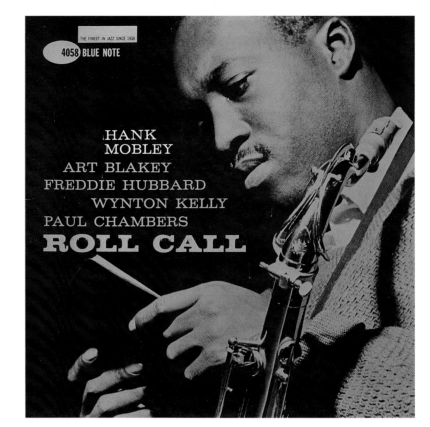

THE FINEST IN JAZZ SINCE 1939
4058 BLUE NOTE

**HANK MOBLEY
ART BLAKEY
FREDDIE HUBBARD
WYNTON KELLY
PAUL CHAMBERS
ROLL CALL**

"SPEAK NO EVIL" 4194
Artist WAYNE SHORTER
Cover Design by REID MILES
Cover Photo by REID MILES

ROLL CALL 4058
Artist HANK MOBLEY
Cover Design by REID MILES
Cover Photo by FRANCIS WOLFF

GEORGE
BRAITH
SOULSTREAM
GRANT GREEN
BILLY GARDNER
HUGH WALKER
STEREO
THE FINEST IN JAZZ SINCE 1939
84161 BLUE NOTE

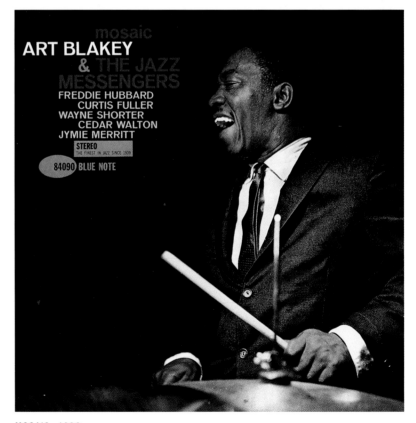

mosaic
ART BLAKEY
& THE JAZZ
MESSENGERS
FREDDIE HUBBARD
CURTIS FULLER
WAYNE SHORTER
CEDAR WALTON
JYMIE MERRITT
STEREO
THE FINEST IN JAZZ SINCE 1939
84090 BLUE NOTE

SOULSTREAM 4161
Artist GEORGE BRAITH
Cover Design by REID MILES
Cover Photo by REID MILES

MOSAIC 4090
Artist ART BLAKEY AND THE JAZZ MESSENGERS
Cover Photo by FRANCIS WOLFF

Opposite: "BREAKING POINT!" 4172 Artist FREDDIE HUBBARD Cover Design by REID MILES Cover Photo by FRANCIS WOLFF

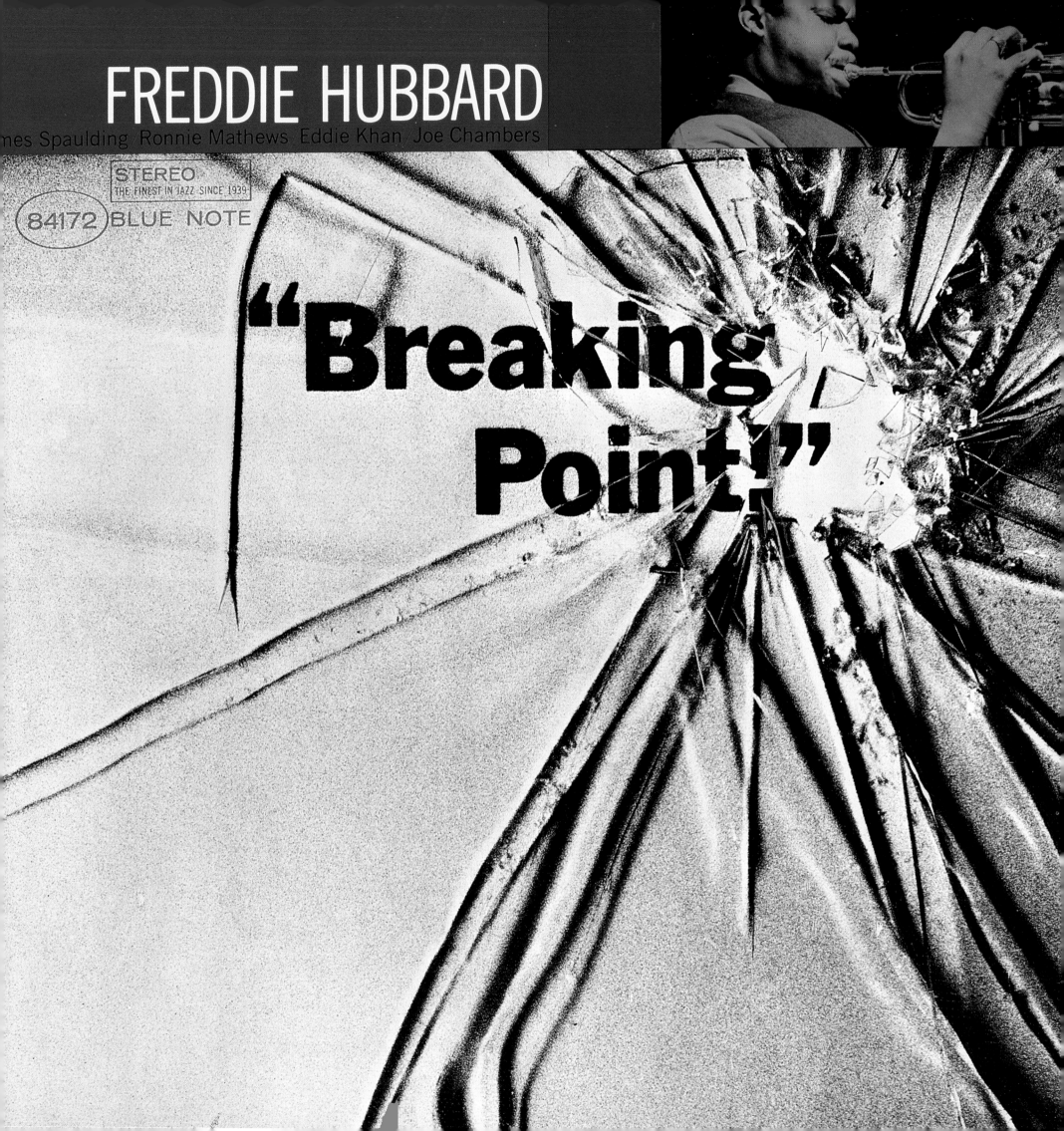

BRING IT HOME TO ME 4228
Artist BLUE MITCHELL
Cover Drawing & Design by GEORGE WRIGHT
Art Direction by REID MILES

HORACE-SCOPE 4042
Artist HORACE SILVER
Cover Drawing by PAULA DONOHUE

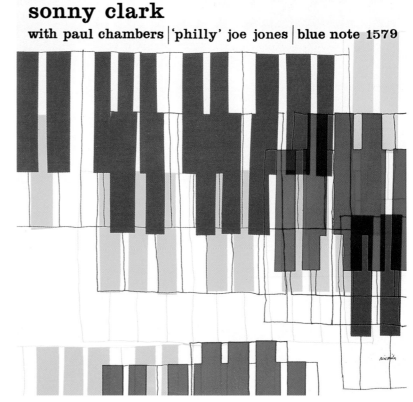

COMPLETE COMMUNION 4226
Artist DON CHERRY
Cover Design by REID MILES
Cover Photo by FRANCIS WOLFF

SONNY CLARK TRIO 1579
Artist SONNY CLARK
Cover Design by REID MILES
Cover Photo by FRANCIS WOLFF

Opposite: BLOWIN' THE BLUES AWAY 4017 Artist HORACE SILVER Cover Design by REID MILES Cover Drawing by PAULA DONOHUE

A NIGHT AT BIRDLAND VOLUME 2 1522
Artist ART BLAKEY QUINTET
Cover Design by REID MILES
Cover Photo by FRANCIS WOLFF

A NIGHT AT BIRDLAND VOLUME 1 1521
Artist ART BLAKEY QUINTET

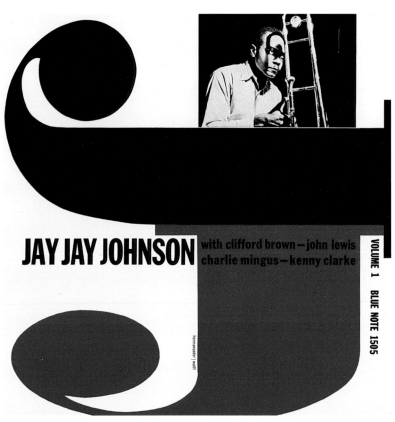

THE EMINENT JAY JAY JOHNSON VOLUME 1 1505
Artist JAY JAY JOHNSON
Cover Design by JOHN HERMANSADER
Cover Photo by FRANCIS WOLFF

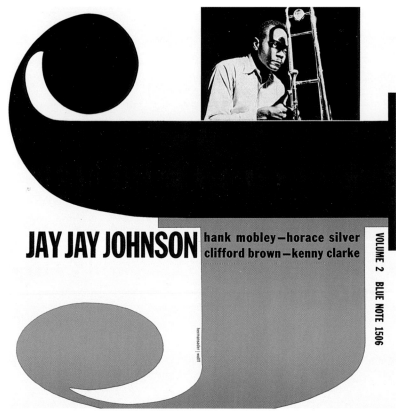

THE EMINENT JAY JAY JOHNSON VOLUME 2 1506
Artist JAY JAY JOHNSON
Cover Design by JOHN HERMANSADER
Cover Photo by FRANCIS WOLFF

Opposite: A NIGHT AT BIRDLAND VOLUME 1 1521 Artist ART BLAKEY QUINTET Cover Design by REID MILES Cover Photo by FRANCIS WOLFF

a night at birdland

ART BLAKEY

jazz corner of the world

CLIFFORD BROWN

LOU DONALDSON

HORACE SILVER   CURLY RUSSELL

ART BLAKEY

THE FINEST IN JAZZ SINCE 1939

BLUE NOTE®

VOLUME 1

LEE MORGAN VOLUME 3 1557
Artist LEE MORGAN
Cover Design by JOHN HERMANSADER
Cover Photo by FRANCIS WOLFF

GOT A GOOD THING GOIN' 4229
Artist JOHN PATTON
Cover Design by REID MILES

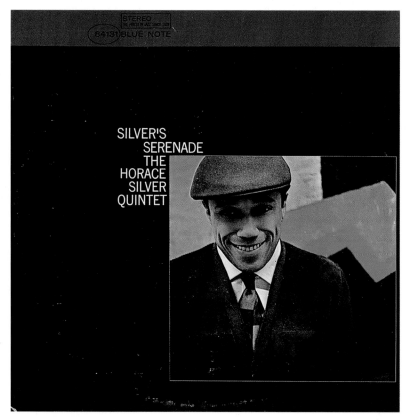

MODE FOR JOE 4227
Artist JOE HENDERSON
Cover Design by REID MILES
Cover Photo by FRANCIS WOLFF

SILVER'S SERENADE 4131
Artist HORACE SILVER
Cover Design by REID MILES
Cover Photo by REID MILES

Opposite: UNIT STRUCTURES 4237 Artist CECIL TAYLOR Cover Design by REID MILES Cover Photo by FRANCIS WOLFF

STEREO

BST 84237

BLP 4237

UNIT STRUC- TURES
CECIL TAYLOR

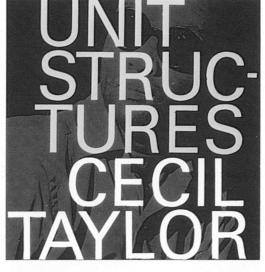

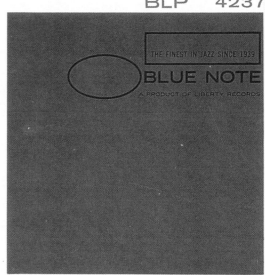

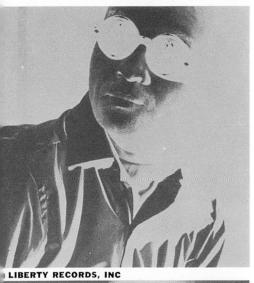

PRINTED IN U.S.A.

RIGHT NOW! 4215
Artist JACKIE McLEAN
Cover Design by REID MILES

"I think typography in the early Fifties
was in a renaissance period anyway. It happened
especially on album covers because
they were not so restrictive as advertising."
REID MILES

A NIGHT IN TUNISIA 4049
Artist ART BLAKEY AND THE JAZZ MESSENGERS
Cover Design by REID MILES
Cover Photo by FRANCIS WOLFF

Opposite: UNITY 4221 Artist LARRY YOUNG Cover Design by REID MILES

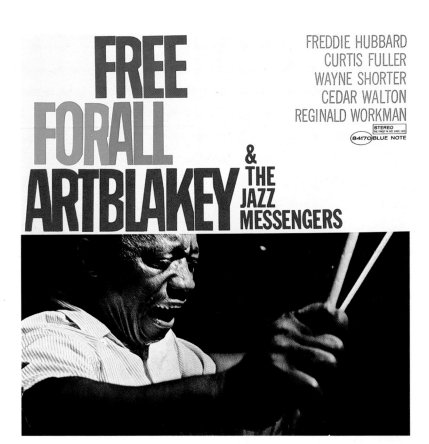

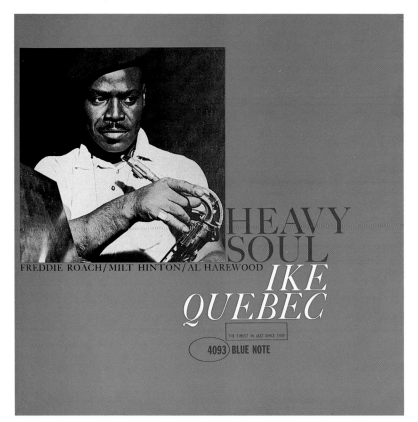

FREE FOR ALL 4170
Artist ART BLAKEY AND THE JAZZ MESSENGERS
Cover Design by REID MILES
Cover Photo by FRANCIS WOLFF

HEAVY SOUL 4093
Artist IKE QUEBEC
Cover Photo by FRANCIS WOLFF

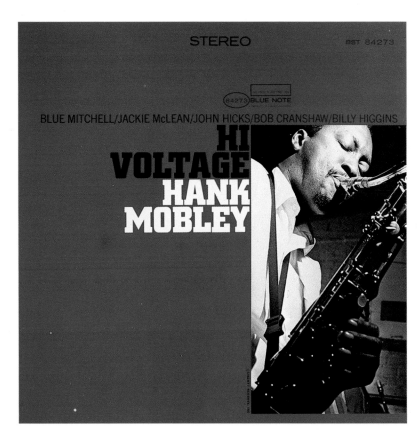

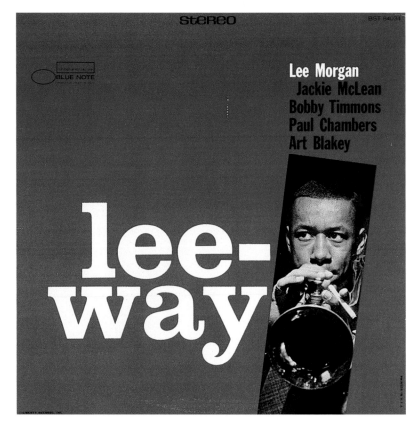

HI VOLTAGE 4273
Artist HANK MOBLEY
Cover Design by REID MILES
Cover Photo by FRANCIS WOLFF

LEE-WAY 4034
Artist LEE MORGAN
Cover Design by REID MILES
Cover Photo by FRANCIS WOLFF

Opposite: DIPPIN' 4209 Artist HANK MOBLEY Cover Design by REID MILES Cover Photo by FRANCIS WOLFF

HANK MOBLEY

LEE MORGAN/HAROLD MABERN, JR./LARRY RIDLEY/BILLY HIGGINS

THE FINEST IN JAZZ SINCE 1939

4209 BLUE NOTE

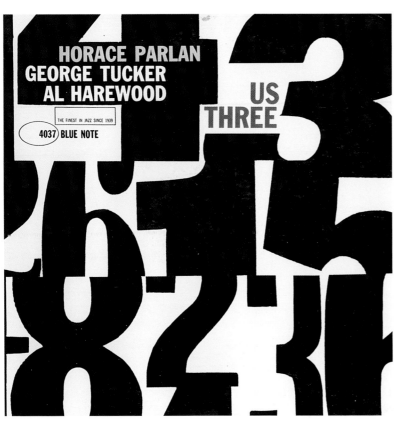

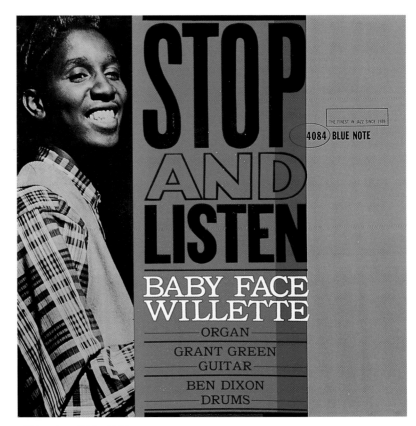

US THREE 4037
Artist HORACE PARLAN
Cover Design by REID MILES

STOP AND LISTEN 4084
Artist BABY FACE WILLETTE
Cover Photo by FRANCIS WOLFF

BYRD IN FLIGHT 4048
Artist DONALD BYRD
Cover Design by REID MILES
Cover Photo by FRANCIS WOLFF

CLIFF JORDAN 1565
Artist CLIFF JORDAN
Cover Design by TOM HANNAN
Cover Photo by FRANCIS WOLFF

Opposite: IN 'N OUT 4166 Artist JOE HENDERSON Cover Design by REID MILES Cover Photo by FRANCIS WOLFF

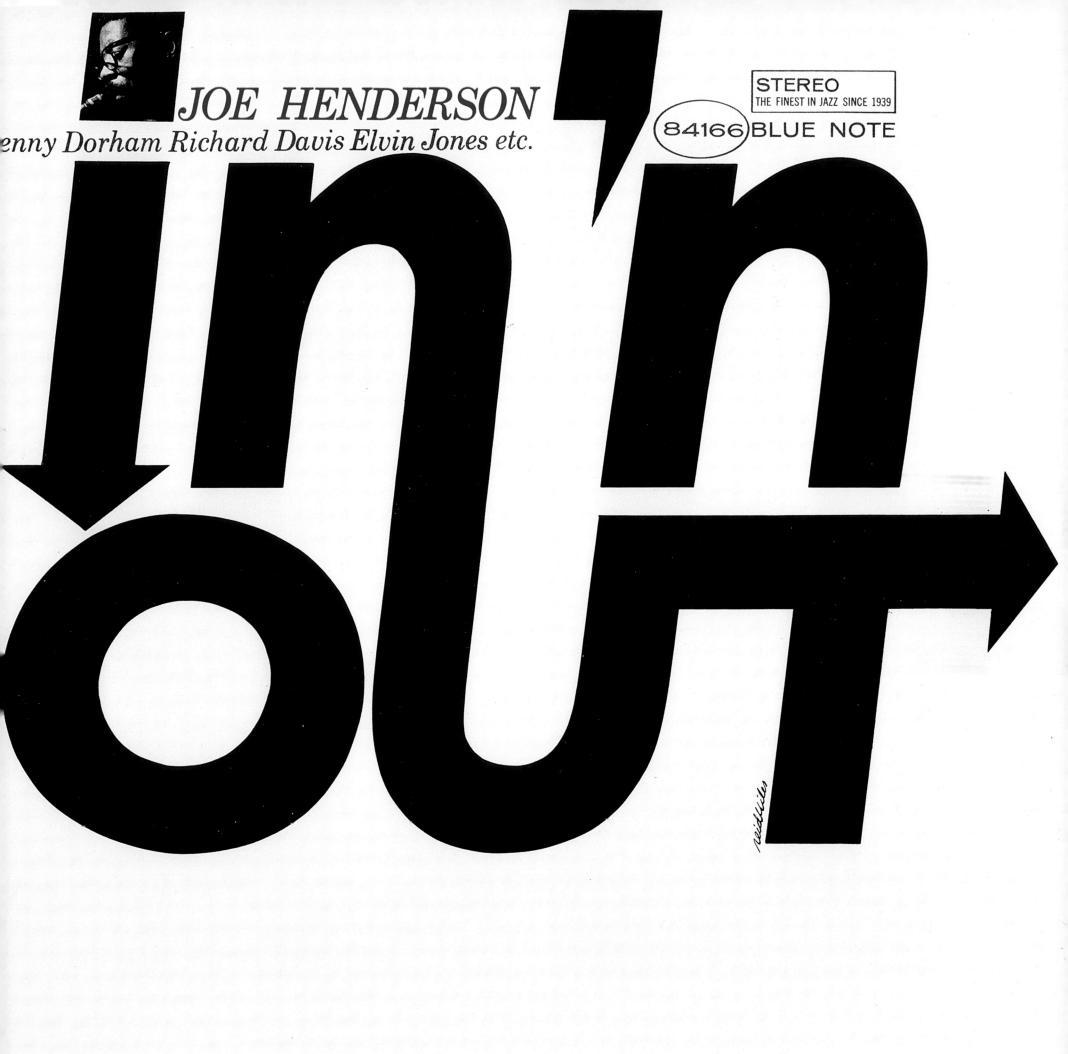

"LET FREEDOM RING" 4106
Artist JACKIE McLEAN
Cover Design by REID MILES
Cover Photo by FRANCIS WOLFF

TALKIN' ABOUT! 4183
Artist GRANT GREEN
Cover Design by REID MILES
Cover Photo by FRANCIS WOLFF

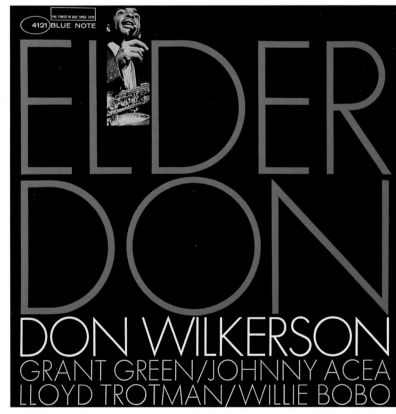

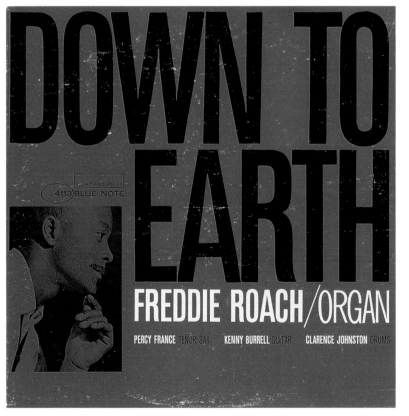

ELDER DON 4121
Artist DON WILKERSON
Cover Design by REID MILES
Cover Photo by FRANCIS WOLFF

DOWN TO EARTH 4113
Artist FREDDIE ROACH
Cover Design by REID MILES
Cover Photo by FRANCIS WOLFF

Opposite: "IT'S TIME!" 4179 Artist JACKIE McLEAN Cover Design by REID MILES Cover Photo by FRANCIS WOLFF

CHARLES TOLLIVER HERBIE HANCOCK CECIL McBEE ROY HAYNES

JACKIE McLEAN

STEREO
THE FINEST IN JAZZ SINCE 1939
84179 BLUE NOTE

"it's time!"...!!!!!!!!!!!!!

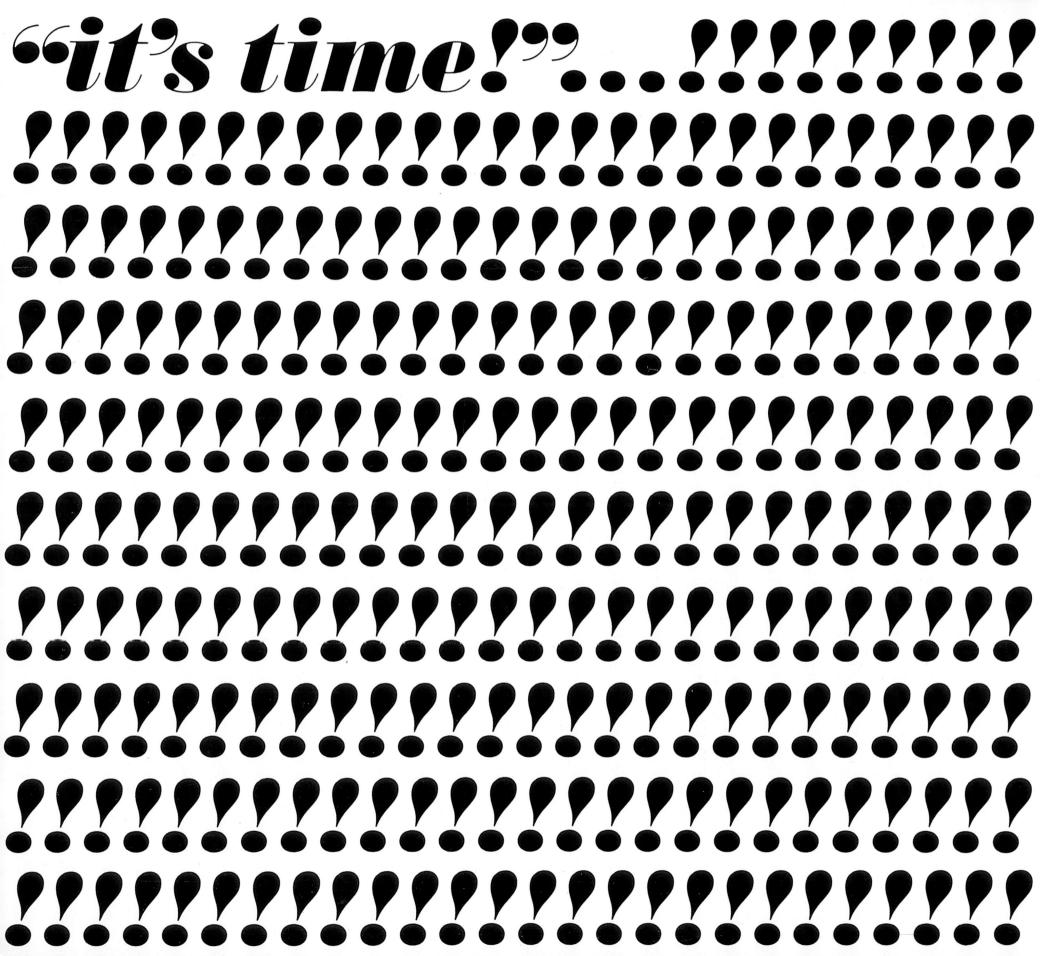

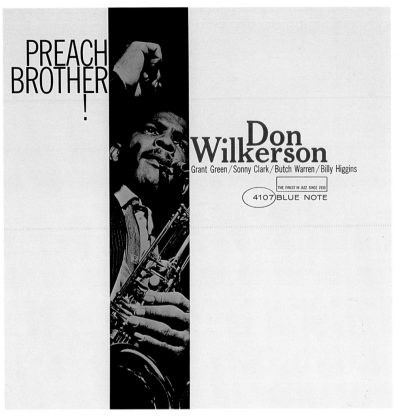

PREACH BROTHER! 4107
Artist DON WILKERSON
Cover Design by REID MILES
Cover Photo by FRANCIS WOLFF

STICK-UP! 4244
Artist BOBBY HUTCHERSON
Cover Design by REID MILES
Cover Photo by FRANCIS WOLFF

NEVER LET ME GO 4129
Artist STANLEY TURRENTINE
Cover Design by REID MILES
Cover Photo by FRANCIS WOLFF

BOSS HORN 4257
Artist BLUE MITCHELL
Cover Design by REID MILES
Cover Photo by FRANCIS WOLFF

Opposite: THE TURNAROUND! 4186 Artist HANK MOBLEY Cover Design by REID MILES Cover Photo by FRANCIS WOLFF

THE TURNAROUND!

FREDDIE HUBBARD BARRY HARRIS PAUL CHAMBERS BILLY HIGGINS

HANK MOBLEY

STEREO
THE FINEST IN JAZZ SINCE 1939
84186 BLUE NOTE

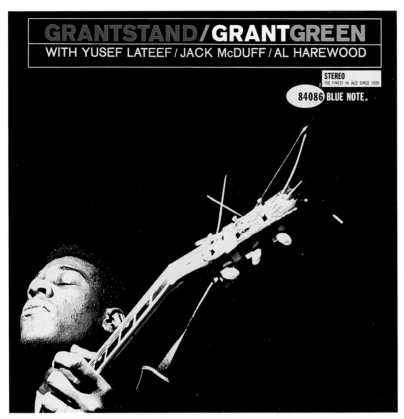

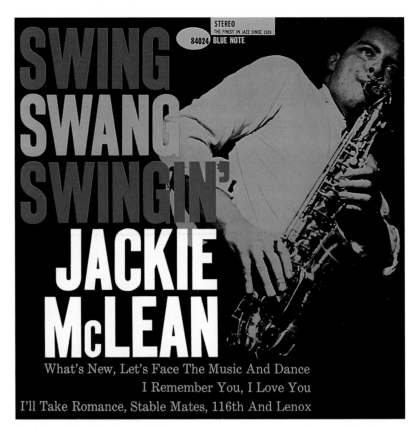

GRANTSTAND 4086
Artist GRANT GREEN
Cover Design by REID MILES
Cover Photo by FRANCIS WOLFF

SWING, SWANG, SWINGIN' 4024
Artist JACKIE McLEAN
Cover Design by REID MILES
Cover Photo by FRANCIS WOLFF

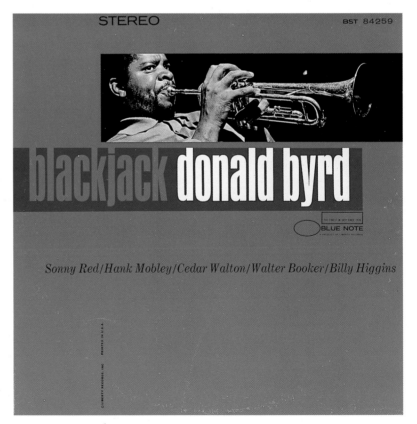

NEW SOIL 4013
Artist JACKIE McLEAN
Cover Design by REID MILES
Cover Photo by FRANCIS WOLFF

BLACKJACK 4259
Artist DONALD BYRD
Cover Design by REID MILES
Cover Photo by FRANCIS WOLFF

Opposite: MIDNIGHT BLUE 4123 Artist KENNY BURRELL Cover Design by REID MILES Cover Photo by FRANCIS WOLFF

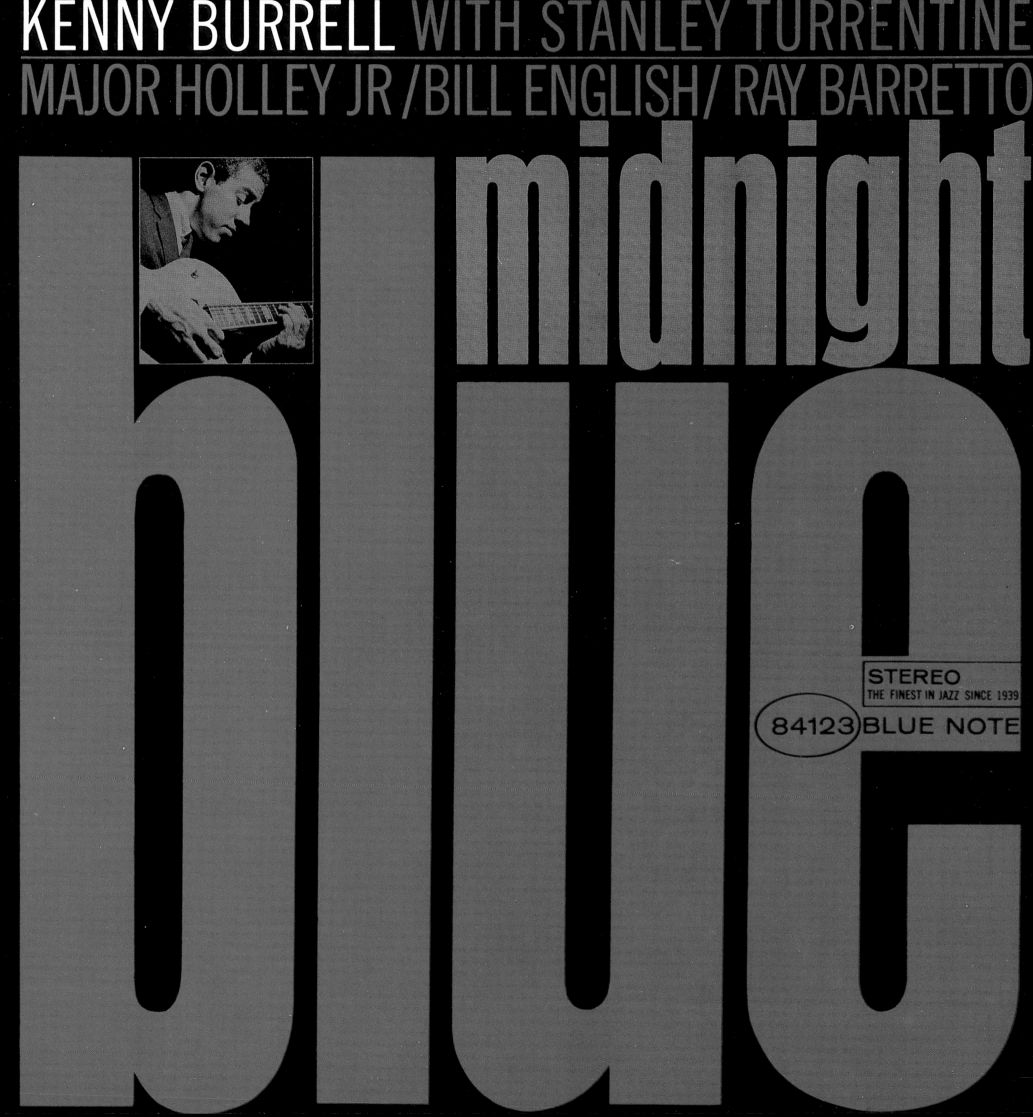

A.T.'s DELIGHT 4047
Artist ART TAYLOR
Cover Design by REID MILES
Cover Photo by FRANCIS WOLFF

THE RUMPROLLER 4199
Artist LEE MORGAN
Cover Design by REID MILES
Cover Photo by FRANCIS WOLFF

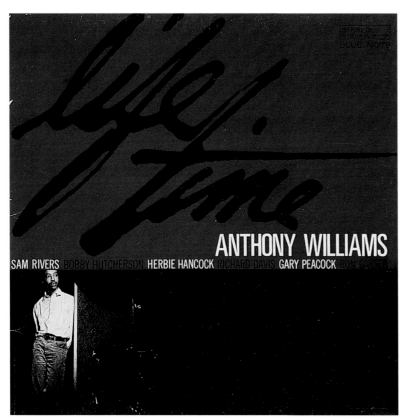

LIFETIME 4180
Artist ANTHONY WILLIAMS
Cover Design by REID MILES
Cover Photo by FRANCIS WOLFF

STREET OF DREAMS 4253
Artist GRANT GREEN
Cover Design by REID MILES
Cover Photo by JIM MARSHALL

Opposite: DESTINATION OUT! 4165 Artist JACKIE McLEAN Cover Design by LARRY MILLER Cover Photo by FRANCIS WOLFF

OUT!

STEREO
THE FINEST IN JAZZ SINCE 1939
84165 BLUE NOTE

Grachan Moncur III | Bobby Hutcherson | Larry Ridley | Roy Haynes

DESTINATION...
JACKIE MC LEAN

CORNBREAD 4222
Artist LEE MORGAN
Cover Design by REID MILES
Cover Photo by FRANCIS WOLFF

"HAPPY FRAME OF MIND"! 4134
Artist HORACE PARLAN
Cover Design by REID MILES
Cover Photo by FRANCIS WOLFF

HERE TO STAY 4135
Artist FREDDIE HUBBARD
Cover Design by REID MILES
Cover Photo by REID MILES

BOSSA NOVA BACCHANAL 4119
Artist CHARLIE ROUSE
Cover Design by REID MILES
Cover Photo by FRANCIS WOLFF

Opposite: TROMPETA TOCCATA 4181 Artist KENNY DORHAM Cover Design by REID MILES Cover Photo by FRANCIS WOLFF

THE FINEST IN JAZZ SINCE 1939

4181 BLUE NOTE

KENNY DORHAM

JOE HENDERSON | TOMMY FLANAGAN | RICHARD DAVIS | ALBERT HEATH

TROMPETA TOCCATA
MAMACITA
NIGHT WATCH
THE FOX

SMITHVILLE 1594
Artist LOUIS SMITH
Cover Photo by FRANCIS WOLFF

DOIN' ALLRIGHT 4077
Artist DEXTER GORDON
Cover Design by REID MILES
Cover Photo by FRANCIS WOLFF

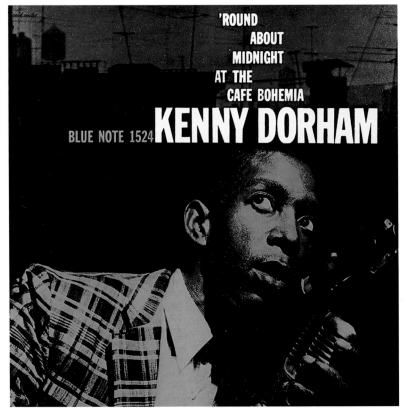

FLIGHT TO JORDAN 4046
Artist DUKE JORDAN
Cover Design by REID MILES
Cover Photo by FRANCIS WOLFF

'ROUND ABOUT MIDNIGHT 1524
Artist KENNY DORHAM
Cover Design by REID MILES
Cover Photo by FRANCIS WOLFF

Opposite: HUB-TONES 4115 Artist FREDDIE HUBBARD Cover Design by REID MILES Cover Photo by FRANCIS WOLFF

james spaulding / herbie hancock / reginald workman / clifford jarvis

hub-tones

STEREO
THE FINEST IN JAZZ SINCE 1939

84115 BLUE NOTE

freddie
hubbard

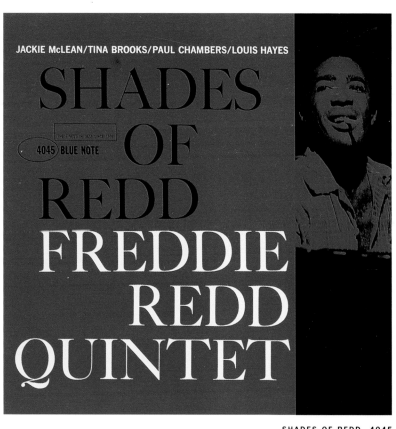

JACKIE McLEAN/TINA BROOKS/PAUL CHAMBERS/LOUIS HAYES

SHADES OF REDD

4045 BLUE NOTE

FREDDIE REDD QUINTET

SONNY'S CRIB **SONNY CLARK**
DONALD BYRD CURTIS FULLER JOHN COLTRANE
PAUL CHAMBERS ART TAYLOR BLUE NOTE 1576

SHADES OF REDD 4045
Artist FREDDIE REDD
Cover Design by REID MILES
Cover Photo by FRANCIS WOLFF

SONNY'S CRIB 1576
Artist SONNY CLARK
Cover Design by REID MILES
Cover Photo by FRANCIS WOLFF

HERBIE
HANCOCK
TAKIN'
OFF
FREDDIE HUBBARD
DEXTER GORDON
BUTCH WARREN
BILLY HIGGINS

STEREO
THE FINEST IN JAZZ SINCE 1939
84109 BLUE NOTE.

STEREO
84189 BLUE NOTE

INNER URGE/JOE HENDERSON

TAKIN' OFF 4109
Artist HERBIE HANCOCK
Cover Design by REID MILES
Cover Photo by REID MILES

INNER URGE 4189
Artist JOE HENDERSON
Cover Design by REID MILES
Cover Photo by FRANCIS WOLFF

Opposite: GO 4112 Artist DEXTER GORDON Cover Design by REID MILES Cover Photo by FRANCIS WOLFF

GO

SONNY CLARK / BUTCH WARREN / BILLY HIGGINS

DEXTER GORDON

STEREO
THE FINEST IN JAZZ SINCE 1939

84112 BLUE NOTE

Stanley Turrentine, Tommy Turrentine, George Tucker, Al Harewood

speakin'
my piece
horace parlan quintet

SPEAKIN' MY PIECE 4043
Artist HORACE PARLAN
Cover Design by REID MILES
Cover Photo by FRANCIS WOLFF

FUCHSIA SWING SONG 4184
Artist SAM RIVERS
Cover Design by REID MILES
Cover Photo by REID MILES

CONTRASTS 4266
Artist LARRY YOUNG
Cover Design by FORLENZA VENOSA DESIGN ASSOCIATES
Cover Photo by FRANCIS WOLFF

"BUCKET"! 4235
Artist JIMMY SMITH
Cover Design by REID MILES
Cover Photo by JEAN-PIERRE LELOIR

Opposite: LITTLE JOHNNY C 4144 Artist JOHNNY COLES Cover Design by REID MILES Cover Photo by FRANCIS WOLFF

little johnny C

THE FINEST IN JAZZ SINCE 1939

4144 BLUE NOTE

Joe Henderson/Duke Pearson
Bob Crenshaw   JOHNNY COLES   TRUMPET
Walter Perkins/Pete La Roca/etc

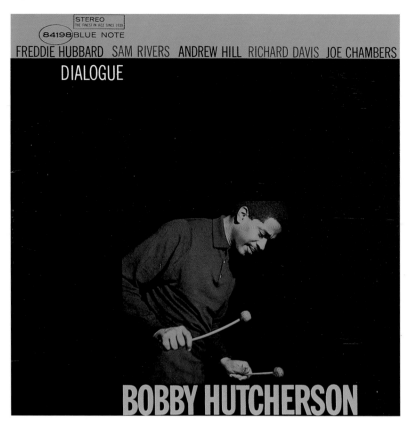

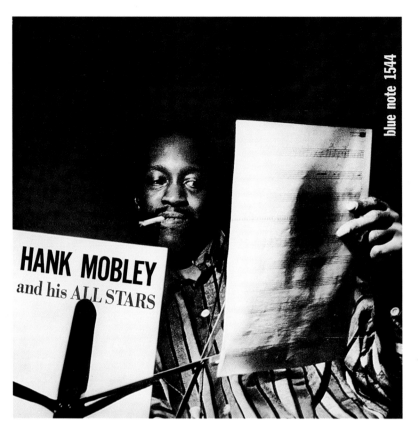

DIALOGUE 4198
Artist BOBBY HUTCHERSON
Cover Design by REID MILES
Cover Photo by FRANCIS WOLFF

HANK MOBLEY AND HIS ALL STARS 1544
Artist HANK MOBLEY
Cover Design by REID MILES
Cover Photo by FRANCIS WOLFF

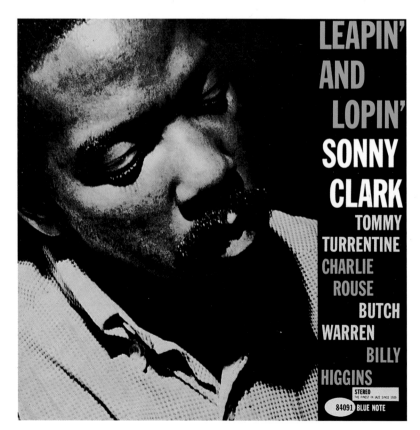

LEAPIN' AND LOPIN' 4091
Artist SONNY CLARK
Cover Photo by FRANCIS WOLFF

A CHIP OFF THE OLD BLOCK 4150
Artist STANLEY TURRENTINE
Cover Design by REID MILES
Cover Photo by REID MILES

Opposite: SOMETHIN' ELSE 1595 Artist CANNONBALL ADDERLEY Cover Design by REID MILES

SOMETHIN' ELSE

CANNONBALL ADDERLEY
MILES DAVIS
HANK JONES
SAM JONES
ART BLAKEY

THE FINEST IN JAZZ SINCE 1939
BLUE NOTE
A PRODUCT OF LIBERTY RECORDS

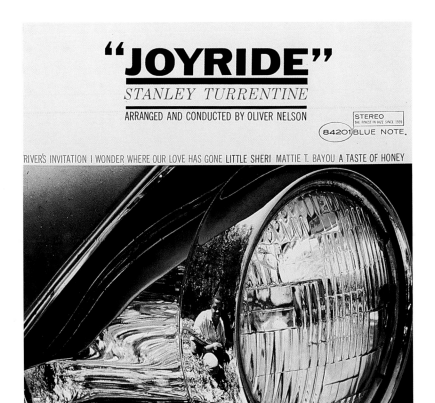

A NEW PERSPECTIVE 4124
Artist DONALD BYRD
Cover Design by REID MILES
Cover Photo by REID MILES

"JOYRIDE" 4201
Artist STANLEY TURRENTINE
Cover Design by REID MILES
Cover Photo by REID MILES

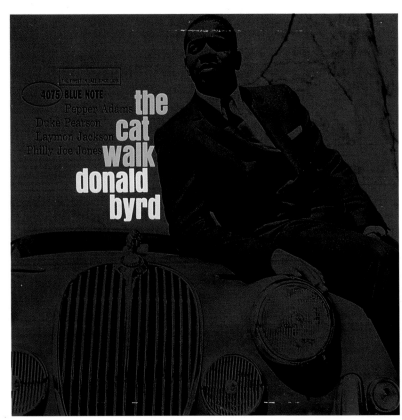

THE CAT WALK 4075
Artist DONALD BYRD
Cover Photo by FRANCIS WOLFF

OFF TO THE RACES 4007
Artist DONALD BYRD
Cover Design by REID MILES
Cover Photo by FRANCIS WOLFF

Opposite: A CADDY FOR DADDY 4230 Artist HANK MOBLEY Cover Design by REID MILES Cover Photo by REID MILES

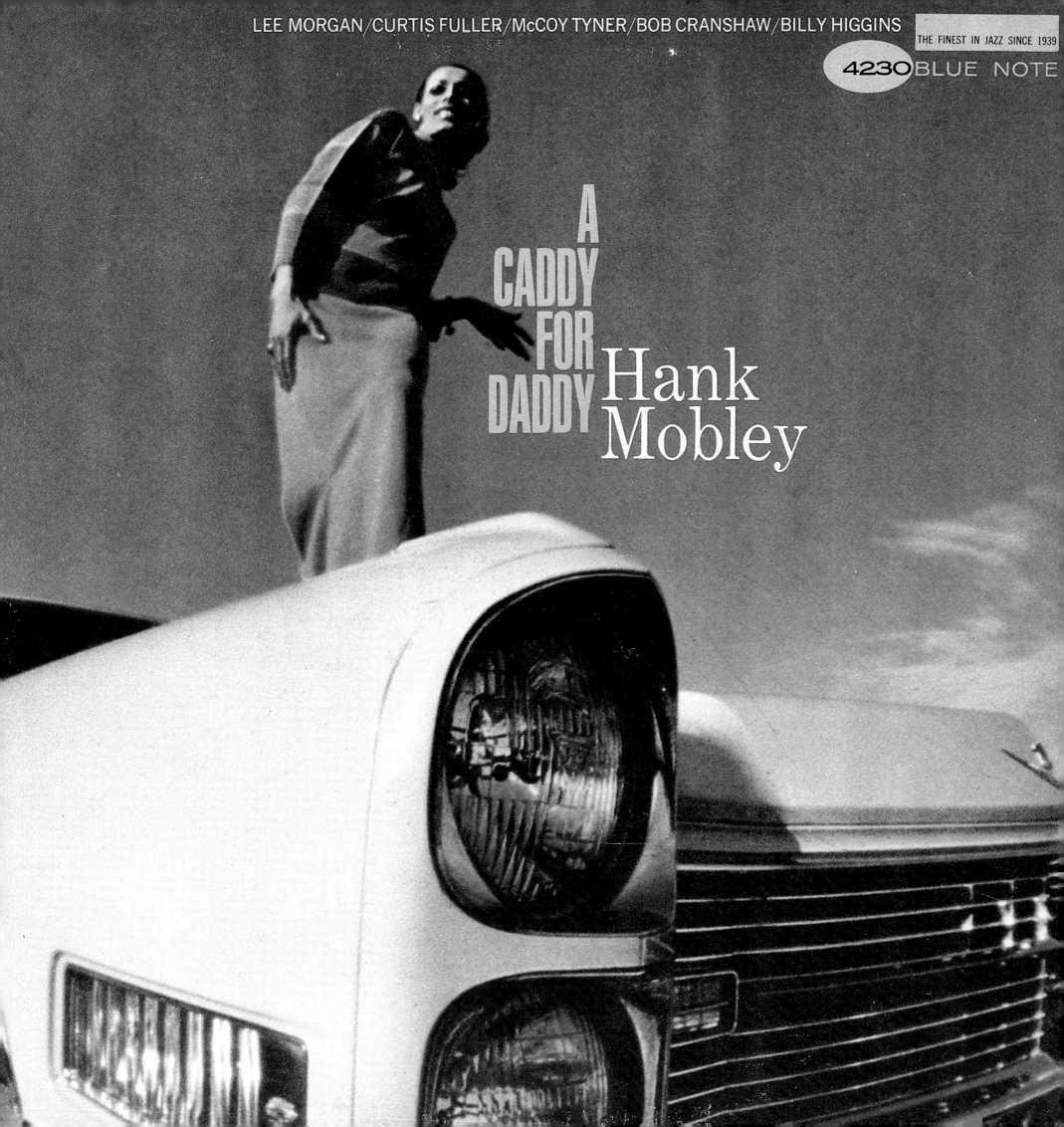

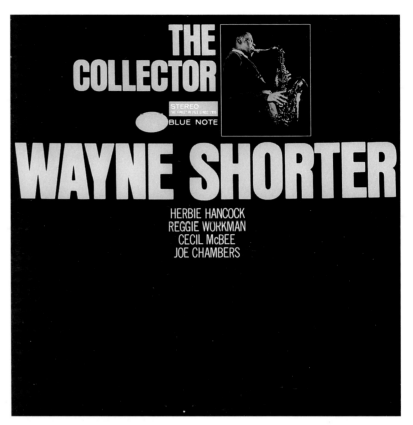

THE COLLECTOR GXF 3059
Artist WAYNE SHORTER
Cover Design by T. FUJIYAMA & A. MIYASHITA

Previously unissued sessions from the Blue Note vaults, released initially in Japan, often had cover designs very much in the tradition laid down by Reid Miles.

POPPIN' GXF 3066
Artist HANK MOBLEY
Cover Photo by K. ABE

Opposite: MATADOR GXF 3053 Artist GRANT GREEN Cover Design & Illustration by T. TANAKA & T. FUJIYAMA

The back covers of Blue Note albums were utilized in a variety of ways. The layout was consistent from album to album throughout the Fifties and Sixties. While sleeve notes predominated, the remaining space could show other available albums either pictorially or in list form. Occasionally photographs of the musicians were used.

BLP-1581/BST-81581

BLUE NOTE

A NIGHT AT THE VILLAGE VANGUARD
SONNY ROLLINS

SONNY ROLLINS, tenor sax; WILBUR WARE, bass; ELVIN JONES, drums;
DONALD BAILEY, bass*; PETE LA ROCA, drums*.   NEW YORK CITY – Nov. 3, 1957.

OLD DEVIL MOON   **SONNYMOON FOR TWO**
SOFTLY AS IN A MORNING SUNRISE   ***A NIGHT IN TUNISIA**
STRIVER'S ROW   **I CAN'T GET STARTED**

— LEONARD FEATHER
(Author of The Book of Jazz)

Cover Photo by FRANCIS WOLFF
Cover Design by REID MILES
Recording by RUDY VAN GELDER

Users of Wide Range equipment should adjust their controls to RIAA curve.

A NIGHT AT THE VILLAGE VANGUARD 1581
Artist SONNY ROLLINS
Cover Design by REID MILES
Cover Photo by FRANCIS WOLFF

HIGH FIDELITY

Blue Note **1580**

THE CONGREGATION
JOHNNY GRIFFIN

JOHNNY GRIFFIN, tenor sax; SONNY CLARK, piano;
PAUL CHAMBERS, bass; KENNY DENNIS, drums.

THE CONGREGATION   **MAIN SPRING**
LATIN QUARTER   **IT'S YOU OR NO ONE**
I'M GLAD THERE IS YOU

JOHNNY GRIFFIN is a symbol of jazz energy.

— ROBERT LEVIN

Cover Design by ANDY WARHOL and REID MILES
Recording by RUDY VAN GELDER

Users of Wide Range equipment should adjust their controls for RIAA curve.

RECENT 12" BLUE NOTE RELEASES

BLP 1530 HORACE SILVER TRIO & ART BLAKEY-SABU
BLP 1531, 1532 ART BLAKEY QUINTET — A NIGHT AT BIRDLAND
BLP 1523 INTRODUCING KENNY BURRELL
BLP 1524 KENNY DORHAM AT THE CAFE BOHEMIA
BLP 1525 THE INCREDIBLE JIMMY SMITH Vol. 1
BLP 1526 CLIFFORD BROWN MEMORIAL ALBUM
BLP 1527 THE MAGNIFICENT THAD JONES
BLP 1528, 1529 THE INCREDIBLE JIMMY SMITH AT CLUB 'BABY GRAND', WILMINGTON, DEL.
BLP 1530 JUTTA HIPP WITH ZOOT SIMS
BLP 1531, 1532 THE FABULOUS FATS NAVARRO
BLP 1533 INTRODUCING JOHNNY GRIFFIN

BLP 1534 PAUL CHAMBERS SEXTET
BLP 1535 KENNY DORHAM OCTET SEXTET
BLP 1536 J. R. MONTEROSE QUINTET
BLP 1537 LOU DONALDSON QUARTET QUINTET SEXTET
BLP 1538 LEE MORGAN INDEED
BLP 1539 HORACE SILVER QUINTET
BLP 1540 HANK MOBLEY WITH DONALD BYRD AND LEE MORGAN
BLP 1541 LEE MORGAN SEXTET
BLP 1542 SONNY ROLLINS QUINTET
BLP 1543 KENNY BURRELL Vol. 2
BLP 1544 HANK MOBLEY AND HIS ALL STARS
BLP 1545 LOU DONALDSON WITH DONALD BYRD
BLP 1546 THE MAGNIFICENT THAD JONES Vol. 3

BLP 1547, 1548 A DATE WITH JIMMY SMITH
BLP 1549 CLIFF JORDAN AND JOHN GILMORE
BLP 1550 HANK MOBLEY WITH ART FARMER
BLP 1551, 1552 JIMMY SMITH WITH DONALDSON, BURRELL, McFADDEN, BLAKEY, BAILEY
BLP 1554, 1555 ART BLAKEY — ORGY IN RHYTHM
BLP 1556 THE SOUNDS OF JIMMY SMITH
BLP 1557 LEE MORGAN Vol. 3
BLP 1558 SONNY ROLLINS WITH JAY JAY, SILVER, MONK, CHAMBERS, BLAKEY
BLP 1559 JOHNNY GRIFFIN WITH MOBLEY, COLTRANE
BLP 1560 HANK MOBLEY SEXTET
BLP 1561 SABU — PALO CONGO

THE CONGREGATION 1580
Artist JOHNNY GRIFFIN
Cover Design by REID MILES & ANDY WARHOL

BLOWIN' THE BLUES AWAY 4017 Artist HORACE SILVER Cover Design by REID MILES Cover Drawing by PAULA DONOHUE

BLOWIN' THE BLUES AWAY
HORACE SILVER QUINTET & TRIO

BLUE MITCHELL, trumpet; JUNIOR COOK, tenor sax; HORACE SILVER, piano;
EUGENE TAYLOR, bass; LOUIS HAYES, drums.

BLOWIN' THE BLUES AWAY
THE ST. VITUS DANCE
BREAK CITY
PEACE

SISTER SADIE
THE BAGHDAD BLUES
MELANCHOLY MOOD   New Version

Finger Poppin' — BLP 4008

Six Pieces of Silver — BLP 1539

HORACE SILVER not only projects a distinct, immediately recognizable talent with his playing but in the way he writes for and guides his group, he again affirmatively expresses his unique personality. In this day of conformity, when many groups are only concerned with "getting a sound", often through gimmickry, Silver's quintet has established their own identity without the aid of spurious musical devices.

Horace does not merely write beginnings and endings for the soloists to fill; he makes his compositions grow by introducing interludes and variations on the opening themes; his ballads have power and yet they are tender: these are some of the reasons that the Silver group does not paint in a monochrome.

Then there is the spirit, the group's emblem which they wear most boldly on the "swingers". "This group has a lot of fire and that's what I want." These words were spoken by leader Silver, one of the fieriest players in jazz. A mild-mannered, sincerely affable young man who dresses with a hip neatness, Horace becomes a perspiring demon when pouring out his musical soul at the piano. I remember Cannonball Adderley, newly arrived in New York, commenting on Horace's off-stand appearance: "How can a cat look one way and then play so funky?"

Apropos of all the talk about "soul" and "funk" recently, it is interesting to note that with Horace Silver, the one who has them in abundant amounts, they have always been natural qualities and never the result of self-conscious striving.

To build a harmony of feeling in a group, you must have musicians who really want to play but the spark must come from the leader. Horace has the unflagging zest which acts as a strong unifying force. In referring to the group's performance level on any given night, he says, "Sometimes we have it, sometimes we don't . . . but nobody ever lays down on the job." This *esprit de corps* gives the quintet a vitality and surging power. Most groups today do not have this necessary ingredient; in the end they sound like pale imitations of one another.

In Blue Mitchell the group has a trumpeter who, while playing within a generally idiomatic style (he has listened to Brownie), says things in his own way. Tenorman Junior Cook, whom I once described as being touched by John Coltrane, is in reality out of the Hank Mobley mold but in a much more muscular manner. Both Blue and Junior have this in common with Horace; they don't waste notes but speak boldly in lean, declarative sentences.

Drummer Louis Hayes, who joined Horace as a teen-ager, has developed into one of the most intelligent of the young, swinging drummers. Eugene Taylor's drive and apartment house-size sound are ex-

plained by Silver: "Gene never has to be coaxed to really work."

The music in this album is the best illustration of all the things I've said about the Horace Silver quintet. The seven numbers, all written by Horace, are excellent representations of his very large talent and the group plays them in the manner to which they have accustomed us.

Blowin' The Blues Away can only be described as a smoker. It has no connection with the number of the same name that Billy Eckstine's band used to play in the '40s.

As in his previous albums, Silver devotes space to his piano in a trio context. *St. Vitus Dance* is the first of two trio tracks here. Horace picked the title for its humor; I doubt if it will make anyone nervous. Spiritually it harks back to some of his first trio offerings on Blue Note.

Break City is so called because of the Charleston-like breaks played by the rhythm section during the theme. This one is another high-caloric cooker.

Peace is for the peaceful mood that it embodies. Horace's titles are as forthright and uncluttered as his music. The writing and playing show the group at their balladic best.

Sister Sadie is from down home. Horace relates that Coltrane, when he heard the group play it in Philly, said to him, "What's the name of that 'amen' number you're playing?"

In the *Baghdad Blues* Silver establishes a Middle Eastern setting. It is not really a blues as far as the changes go, but has much of the blues feeling in the minor mode.

The second trio track, *Melancholy Mood*, was originally heard in a first version as part of *Further Explorations By The Horace Silver Quintet* (Blue Note 1589). Its further exploration was brought about by pianist Gil Coggins playing of it at Horace's house. "The other version was out-of-tempo with Teddy Kotick bowing behind me. Gilly played it out-of-tempo too, but with some new voicings that inspired me to try a different interpretation of the tune and play it in tempo," explains Horace.

If this album doesn't succeed in blowing your blues away, then I doubt whether you ever really had them in the first place.

— IRA GITLER

Cover Drawing by PAULA DONOHUE
Cover Design by REID MILES
Recording by RUDY VAN GELDER

Blue Mitchell performs by courtesy of Riverside Records.

Users of Wide Range equipment should adjust their controls for RIAA curve.

Horace Silver and The Jazz Messengers — BLP 1518

Further Explorations – BLP 1589

the stylings of SILVER

The Stylings of Silver — BLP 1562

Horace Silver Trio with Art Blakey - Sabu – BLP 1520

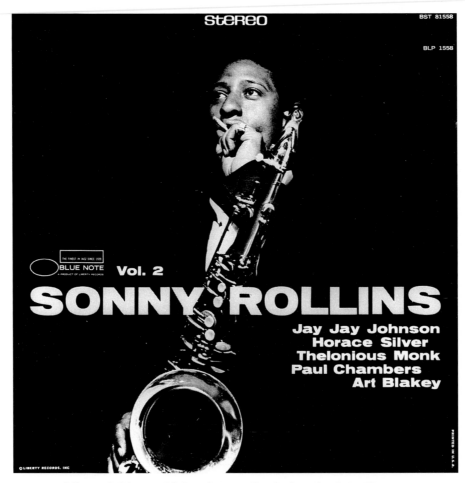

All good things which exist are the fruits of originality . . .

... Imitation is the sincerest form of flattery.

Lee Morgan with John Coltrane at *Blue Train* session; 1957

Opposite: Alfred Lion and Art Blakey; 1956

Alfred Lion and Sonny Clark at rehearsal; August 23, 1957

Alfred Lion and Freddie Hubbard

Clifford Brown in his debut session with Gigi Gryce; 1953

Tony Williams at BN session; 1963

Opposite: Curtis Fuller and Bud Powell on the *Bud!* session; 1957

Alfred Lion and Dexter Gordon in the early '60s

Opposite: Herbie Hancock at BN session; 1962

124

DOWN BEAT magazine November 1961

DOWN BEAT magazine May 1965

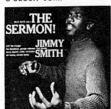

125

INTERNATIONALLY FAMOUS

ART BLAKEY
& THE JAZZ MESSENGERS

just returned from a triumphal tour of EUROPE (France, Belgium, Germany, Holland, Sweden, Denmark and Switzerland) and a smash success in JAPAN.

JUST RELEASED!

A NIGHT IN TUNISIA   **ART BLAKEY**
With Lee Morgan, Wayne Shorter, Bobby Timmons, Jymie Merritt
A Night In Tunisia, Sincerely Diana, So Tired, Yama, Kozo's Waltz

BLUE NOTE 4049

THE BIG BEAT   BLP 4029*

AT "THE JAZZ CORNER OF THE WORLD"   BLP 4015/16*

AT BIRDLAND   BLP 1521/22

MOANIN'   BLP 4003*

AT THE CAFE BOHEMIA   BLP 1507/08

12" LP List $4.98—Stereo $5.98   *Also available in Stereo   √ Free Catalog On Request

BLUE NOTE RECORDS INC., • 43 West 61st Street, New York 23, N.Y.

DOWN BEAT magazine March 1961

INDEX OF ARTISTS

great songs... of the sixties

volume 1

edited by **milton okun**

introduction by **tom wicker**

Cherry Lane Music Company
• *Quality In Printed Music* •
6 East 32nd Street, New York, NY 10016

EXCLUSIVELY DISTRIBUTED BY

HAL•LEONARD®
CORPORATION

7777 W. BLUEMOUND RD. P.O. BOX 13819 MILWAUKEE, WI 53213

CONTENTS

To my parents, Will and Leah Okun

Acknowledgements
I would like to express my sincerest thanks to the following friends and associates for their
unstinting help and suggestions: Al Brackman, John Denver, Leslie Elliott, Ronald Feldman,
Karen Fortney, Victoria Heller, Arch Lustberg, Adam Nagourney, Ed Ochs, Ellen Sander, and especially
my sister-in-law, Jean Dinegar, who has brought new meaning to the word nepotism.

I would also like to thank the fraternity of music publishers whose generous
and gracious cooperation has made this collection possible.

Milton Okun

great songs... of the sixties

volume 1

of the sixties

Milton Okun The Sixties: Song and Sound

...A song has a few rights,
The same as other ordinary citizens.
If it feels like walking along the left-hand side of the street,
Passing the door of physiology
Or sitting on the curb,
Why not let it?
If it feels like kicking over an ashcan,
A poet's castle,
Or the prosodic law,
Will you stop it?

— Charles Ives.

In the 1960's, American popular music rocked to an explosion whose echoes are still being heard around the world. It reverberated with new energy, vibrancy and genius. Never before had the thriving field of American popular song been so bold in subject matter or so infused with creative talent.

The romantic love song, polished to a mellow gleam, was the mainstay of the pop music field of the Thirties and Forties and Fifties, one whose proved record Tin Pan Alley was loath to part with. Though incorporating passing trends in bebop and rhythm and blues, the professionals were secure in their formula of moon-June-spoon.

But the decade of the Sixties moved to the intense beat of a young, passionate generation. The writers were perhaps less sophisticated and certainly less professional than craftsmen like the Gershwins, Porter, Kern, Hammerstein, Rodgers and Hart, Harburg and Berlin. These writers, the best of Tin Pan Alley, impressed us with their skill, their clever way with words, their ability to work and rework that same old feeling. But we could hardly believe that they were expressing their own feelings. Their songs dealt with a single emotion —romantic love—in a way that seems superficial and impersonal. The young Sixties generation, on the other hand, was desperately concerned with the quality of life—and this concern marked the departure of popular music from sentimentality to hard reality.

The explosion originated in a varied set of musical fires previously outside the ken of popular song. The most important was Negro music, with its gospel intensity, its rhythmic freedom and drive, and its human, realistic vocal styles. Perhaps it wasn't pretty or cute or sweetly melodic, but it had real gut emotion. People sang as they really felt, so there were many more vocal possibilities. The cry, the laugh and the sneer had musical expression— it was called Soul.

Another current that fed the new creativity was the folk revival. Henry Pleasants in Serious Music—and All That Jazz! describes the discovery of folk music by the young Americans of the post-World War II generation as possibly "the healthiest thing that had happened in music in several hundred years. Young musical America—its requirements and its tastes ignored by the professionals of both the Serious and the jazz communities— *simply took music into its own hands* (italics mine). And it produced, in due course, its own professionals—Bob Dylan, Joan Baez, Simon and Garfunkel and many others."

Traditionally, in folk music there has been no limitation of subject matter. Everything that concerned people could be found in this music: birth, death, anger, love (of all kinds, not merely romantic). People sang and created to express their feelings, not to feed a commercial market. In the Sixties, this new generation of writers overturned the commercial restraints on subject matter and taste, and created an art form that is one of the most important cultural revolutions in history.

These songs constitute a body of work that has significance beyond its entertainment value and commercial success. They mark a sharp qualitative change from the pop music of earlier decades. The music represents the life style and point of view of the new generation that produced it, a generation whose motivation and creative urges could better compare to those of the classic and romantic composers of the Eighteenth and Nineteenth Centuries than to those of Tin Pan Alley.

The new writers have expanded the accepted meaning of love far beyond the merely personal and romantic. It now deals with our feeling about people, all people, humankind, the problems of life, the need for tenderness. The songwriters are not fabricating a product for a market. They are creating out of their guts and pain and anger. Some of it isn't polished. Much of it is weak. But an amazing proportion of it is of an intensity and anguish that has made this popular music a major art form.

The number of fine songs written in the 1960's and the multiplicity of styles and audiences made the selection of songs for this book difficult. This was not to be a collection of the editor's favorites (although it is undoubtedly limited by his prejudices). It is intended as a cross-section of the myriad musical talents and directions of these years.

The music of the Sixties was *sound* as much as *song*. And the big sound was rock.

What are the musical characteristics of rock? How does it differ from standard pop music? What basically happened was that the rhythm section, consisting of bass, guitar, drums and piano, which formerly gave the underpinning to a band, stepped to the front and became the whole band. Where before each member of the rhythm section had a different function, in rock the group united, formed a battering ram and became a powerful and fluid entity. For example, previously the bass would play only the most fundamental of chord tones, almost always on the first beat or the first and third beats of each measure. It was truly the bottom of the music, always there, always predictable. Now the bass, electrically amplified rather than acoustic, plays as a guitar or drum might, in constantly varying rhythmic patterns.

Prior to rock, the guitar would perform its two functions, either rhythm "chicks" on the second and fourth beats of the measure, or melodic "riffs" that would fill the spaces at the ends of vocal phrases. Rock guitaring expanded these rhythmic and melodic functions, mainly by utilizing a much wider sound spectrum. Guitars were developed, electrically and structurally, to play in such varied tone colors that often they were not recognized as guitars. Instead of short riffs, long melodic improvisations became guitar style.

The drummer's function also changed. Formerly, drum technique was between the left and right hands, with the bass drum, when hit by the foot, giving a relatively subtle one-two-three-four. In rock drumming, there is close coordination between the left hand on the snare drum and the right foot on the bass drum, playing a less subtle and very free strong rhythm. The right hand hits the ride cymbal and the left foot the high hat or sock cymbal. Where the accents used to be almost solely on two and four, now they are on one, two, three and four, plus everything in between. In the past, the drummer had to wait for his solo to shine, but now he goes at it all the time. He is continually in the center of the action.

Since the bassist no longer restricts himself to the fundamental tones of the chord, but plays extended rhythmic figures, he can work very closely with the drummer. They often play in tandem, forcing the rhythm into prominence. These rhythmic figures, particularly when the guitar is added, become strong physical impulses. Since the musicians can ignore their former varied responsibilities in backing a band, they can become a free force that can go in any direction. Each instrument can work in a solo or to reinforce the others.

Rhythm like this must be worked out in rehearsal. It is much more complex and demanding than the reading of standard rhythm charts. Since most of the excitement comes from rhythmic development, plus improvisation, the trained arranger is not needed. Now there is arranging by group. One by-product of rock thus has been the unemployment of arrangers.

As much time, energy and imagination go into the recording of songs as into their writing and arrangement. Electronic equipment, with its vast new technical resources of multi-track recording, allows and encourages new concepts. All the methods and rules of the previous generation are discarded. For example, distortion is no longer the hobgoblin of recording. It is used to bring out new qualities of sound with new physical impact.

The imaginative use of the electronic facilities of the studios is due, in large part, to the fact that the song creators now make their own records. They look for more and more ways to highlight the feel of their music. In the Forties and Fifties, the greatest expense in recording was for musicians and arrangements. In the rock period, it is the cost of studio facilities that is the larger. Since schooling has become less critical, music making is open to many more people. The parallel development of multi-track tape recording fits in very well with the opening of the field to these relatively untrained performers. In multi-track recording, one person can record many different parts, instrumental or vocal, on the same tape. One person could literally play an entire symphony or opera by recording each track himself, later mixing the tracks to get the final result.

It would be impossible to assess the songs of the Sixties without discussing some of its most influential and representative creative talents. The list must be headed by The Beatles. What attracted so many to this improbable young quartet from Liverpool was their humor. But it was their music, combining the influences of American black and white music, that caught on and gave them great success.

What proved most surprising, however, was that they didn't relax into a given style but proceeded to find new ways of writing, performing, recording. They became the most important single influence on popular music in history. Each Beatle album had its own delights—new approaches to arranging and songs of greater and greater creativity. As a result, the most difficult task I had in editing this book was to choose the four songs that were to represent John Lennon and Paul McCartney.

I Want to Hold Your Hand was chosen for historical reasons. It was the first giant hit that brought The Beatles to the world's attention. I remember the excitement of first hearing it, the dash and energy of the octave jump to the word "hand," the freedom of the singing, its strong (at that time) dissonance.

Eleanor Rigby is a song of such individuality that it represents Lennon and McCartney at the high point of their creativity and uniqueness. It is musically and structurally innovative and has lyrics of intense poignancy.

Hey Jude exemplifies the inability to separate the music of the Sixties from many of its composers-as-performers. The single recording of this particular song—at an unprecedented seven minutes of running time—has been one of the greatest sellers in recording history. Yet the sheet music doesn't reflect the fascinating complexity of the song as recorded by The Beatles.

Yesterday is the one song that everyone agreed upon as belonging in this collection. Many people call it the finest ballad of this entire period. No one imagined on first seeing The Beatles, a wild and free-wheeling rock group, that they would come to produce a song of such beauty and richly textured harmony.

There was a giant counterpoint to the melody of The Beatles: Bob Dylan. They quickly came to understand this and treated Dylan as a separate but equal talent. They were influenced by many artists, but by none as consciously as Dylan. Dylan himself had an impact on the American cultural scene second to none. As a performer, he was not accepted as widely and enthusiastically as were The Beatles. He was not the humorous, crowd-pleasing, fun-loving entertainer that it would have taken to match The Beatles. Instead, he was a sharp, incisive, political spokesman for an entire generation. His harsh realities and uncompromising challenges tended to alienate everyone but the young. It is Dylan's music that gave the generation gap its focus and the new generation its voice.

In June 1970, Bob Dylan was given an honorary degree by Princeton University. He was described as "one of the most popular musicians of the last decade. He has based his techniques in the arts of the common people of our past and torn his appeals for human compassion from the experience of the dispossessed. Although he is now approaching the perilous age of 30, his music remains the authentic expression of the disturbed and concerned conscience of America."

A fascinating aspect of Dylan's career has been its constant change of direction. It reminds me most of the career of Pablo Picasso—when the public finally accepted Picasso's new style, after initially having rejected it, he was off in a new direction, earning a new rejection. In 1965 when Dylan dominated the folk field, he abruptly switched his musical style to electric rock. In his initial rock performances, the audiences, which had come to cheer him, booed.

Not enough attention has been paid to Dylan's musicianship. His use of dissonance is bold and imaginative. His melodies are simple and often elegant in their line.

The songs of Dylan in this collection include the two most important political statements of the decade—*The Times They Are A-Changin'*, an angry challenge to the older generation, and *Blowin' In The Wind*, a song of gentle despair.

Paul Simon, perhaps more than any other single writer, represents the latent genius of young America. The imagery, poetry and subtlety of his writing, combined with passion and involvement, have formed a body of work that has no parallel in the writings of earlier American songwriters. Simon has caught the feelings of alienation of youth as no one else has.

The Dangling Conversation is a gem of delicacy and insight. Before the Sixties that kind of lyric—or that of *The Sound of Silence*—would have been unacceptable in popular music. There just weren't lyrics that could be understood on so many levels. *Mrs. Robinson*—a stinging, perceptive comment on American society—is another song with a lyric of courage and sharpness.

None of Simon's earlier works prepared us for the heartbreaking loveliness of *Bridge Over Troubled Water*. It has the simplicity of a beautiful hymn—at the same time, its harmonic progressions and soaring melody are reminiscent of the lyrical moments in Verdi and Puccini.

A songwriting team whose music and lyrics seem an extension and development of the best of previous American popular music is Burt Bacharach and Hal David. Bacharach, a musician of great charm and ability, and David, a consummate lyricist, wrote a series of very successful songs in the Sixties which can be characterized as imaginative, direct though often complex, and respectful of the intelligence of their audiences. Bacharach's music breaks the rules of the popular song past. Irregular meters, unusual and provocative harmonic patterns, and especially an almost Mozartean element of surprising melodic direction all add up to music of wit and originality.

David's lyrics have a strength that is equal to the music's demands. His writing is sharp, lean and devoid of clichés. If you read through the lyrics of *Alfie* and the three other songs that represent Bacharach and David in this book—*Walk On By, What the World Needs Now Is Love* and *Raindrops Keep Fallin' on My Head*—you will understand why Hal David is considered such a master craftsman.

While all of the songs in this book were not hits (I have yet to meet anyone who knows every song in the book), wherever there was a choice between a fine song that had not achieved public recognition and one that had, I chose the better-known song. After all, this is a collection to be played and sung and familiarity helps in playing and singing.

Perhaps my evaluation of the new music is too extravagant, but it seems clear now that it has struck the kind of responsive chord that the previous songwriters had never touched. The music has become international in scope. It has evolved within the last fifteen years from being merely dance music to being an inspiration, an obsession, and an important focus of commitment for the young intellectuals of the world.

The songs in this book are, in a way, the musical accompaniment to the real life and times of the Sixties. They form a varied score to go along with a decade of disillusionment, violence, unrest, uncertainty and unparalleled scientific accomplishments. They counterpoint a human revolution in morality and civil rights. They reflect the dominance of youth and the young sound in a period of time when a new search has begun to define the importance of man and his place in the scheme of things.

Tom Wicker Arcadia and Aquarius

Some believe it really was the dawning of the Age of Aquarius, the beginning of an era of
   ...harmony and understanding,
   sympathy and trust abounding,
   no more falsehoods or derisions,
   golden living dreams of visions,
   mystic crystal revelation
   and the mind's true liberation...
and thus they said the decade of the Sixties heralded a time when
   ...peace will guide the planets
   and love will steer the stars.

   This idyllic view could be made momentarily plausible to even the most jaded audience (despite some reservations as to how the mind should be liberated) by the frenetic young cast of "Hair," the American Tribal Love-Rock Musical, a Broadway show that my daughter informed me "everyone ought to be required to see" and which stands with Woodstock as symbols of the flower-child experience of the Sixties.

   But the older you were, and the more weary, the shorter the hold the Aquarius notion was likely to have. Less mindblowing but still optimistic was the view of Senator Eugene McCarthy, the Pied Piper of Political Participation. With many others, he saw the decade as a sort of solemn national revival in which youthful evangelists equipped with "intelligence, a deep sense of moral responsibility, an openness of spirit and hope" made "deep, even dangerous commitments." And that meant that "in retrospect the Sixties will be distinguished as the decade in which the spirit of America, largely through its young people, was renewed and revitalized."

   Others were not so sanguine, as they watched President Richard M. Nixon usher in the Seventies. Not a few mothers, before and after seeing "Hair," looked at their offspring and wondered with Tevye and Golde of Anatevka:
   Is this the little girl I carried?
   Is this the little boy at play?
   I don't remember growing older,
   When did they?

   And there were also those who found champions in Governor Ronald Reagan or Vice President Spiro T. Agnew—who saw the "revolution" of the Sixties as a menace to American traditions, democratic ideals, and property values. Some spoke darkly of parallels to the conditions that spawned Nazi Germany; the national commission on civil disorders warned of "two nations, separate, and unequal"—black and white. And why not, voices kept asking plaintively throughout a decade of marching and alarm, talk about what's right with America?

   So those were the days, my friend, we thought they'd never end, but what did they really mean, if anything? What *were* the Sixties all about, other than the age-old phenomena of man, tears and laughter and love and hate and the melancholy of time passing...*oh my friends we're older but no wiser.* After all, for many, life in the Sixties was, as always, a cabaret, even if we *were* waist deep in the Big Muddy; and if still others had to live in the profound faith that we shall overcome, for want of anything better to believe, they at least had John Kennedy to remind them that life is inherently unfair.

   I am not sure you can find the meaning of a time, if it had one, in its music, and this book of songs makes the point. Let us suppose that The Beatles, some of whose work is, authorities say, "as carefully constructed as a Mozart quartet," made the authentic sound of the Sixties. One might draw a conclusion from that; but what would he then do with

Where Have all the Flowers Gone? or Nashville or Aretha Franklin or *My Way* bellowed by a travesty of what used to be Frank Sinatra when I was learning to jitterbug at the high school gym thirty years ago? The Beatles were probably the best we had in the Sixties, but the musical expression of the decade? One could as accurately say that in politics it was L.B.J.'s Voting Rights Act, which might also have been the best we had, but didn't begin to symbolize the Sixties. There is just too much of a decade—politically, musically, socially, in every way—to pin down.

But surely it can be said that certain music inevitably reflects certain aspects of a certain time. It interests me that much of the music of the Sixties—including most of the songs I've mentioned—hangs on some aspect of *change,* even when they don't seem to. The mystery of what the girl and Billy Joe threw off the Tallahatchee Bridge means less to me than the revelation in the last verse that it was all in the past, time has gone by— sad reflections, new circumstances, brother's off to Tupelo with a bride—*change.* And the reason that

> *...one man, scorned and covered with scars,*
> *still strove with his last ounce of courage*
> *to reach the unreachable stars...*

was that "the world will be better for this." Again, *change.* I am willing to link that word to the Sixties, but not many others, and it seems to me that Bob Dylan may have described the decade best:

> *There's a battle*
> *Outside and it's ragin'*
> *It'll soon shake your windows*
> *And rattle your walls.*

Dylan was not referring to Vietnam, at least not exclusively. Vietnam was not so much the battle itself as the distant artillery rumble that finally woke some of us to what Dylan had been trying to convey. The times, they were a-changin'—more swiftly and more profoundly than ever before, and *that* was the battle, that was the central experience of the Sixties, whether one urged it on and welcomed it, or resisted and lamented. And it came to us all.

Change arrived in so many guises in the Sixties that it was difficult to tell what mattered and what was superficial or faddish. When American young men opted more widely than at any time since the Civil War for long hair and beards, no doubt the basic impulse was rebellion against the crew-cut, gray-flannel, suburban-house conformity of post-war America

> *And the children go to school,*
> *and the children go to summer camp,*
> *and then to the university*
> *where they are put in boxes*
> *and they all come out the same...*
> *and they're all made out of ticky-tacky*
> *and they all look just the same.*

Yet, the hairy look itself soon came to be a kind of orthodoxy, as did all those denim pants, Indian beads and sandals. The sudden immense popularity of pro football on television probably had some psychological derivation from the violence of the times, as often argued, but pro boxing went virtually off the air, and what about the sudden immense popularity of pro golf? What probably mattered most, in each case, was that the pace of pro football was naturally swift, and the networks cut out most of the preliminaries and also-rans in the big golf tournaments and focused on the closing holes and contending players for a fast, dramatic show; thus, these sports, like the times, *moved.* Most of the boxers we saw in the Fifties on Fight of the Week seldom did.

Minor change sometimes suggested deeper change. When the Supreme Court outlawed prayer in the public schools, that was not intrinsically so great a matter; religion in America had never been dependent on the schools and many denominations actively supported the strict separation of church and state. Yet, the Court's action came at a time of precipitous decline for church influences in American life, and seemed to symbolize the emergence of a new way of life—rationalist and enlightened to some, hedonist and decadent to others —*change* to both.

Other movement was ambiguous. The miniskirt, perhaps, was only part of the long-established ability of the master salesmen of the *couture* to put hemlines down or up at will; yet, the ladies were showing more of themselves than ever before in other ways, too— bikinis, see-through blouses, discarded underwear—even while the strongest feminist movement since Susan B. Anthony was emerging at the end of the decade. Development of The Pill, as well as the national movement towards more easily avaliable abortions, obviously had profound implications, but which was most important—that they tended to set women free to enjoy sex as never before, or that they tended to set women free from the dominance of children and the men who fathered them? Or was that the same thing? In the Sixties, it was only possible to be sure that the world of the female was undergoing metamorphosis perhaps even more than that of the male.

Other changes really were developments from a familiar past. In music, the rise of rock was phenomenal, as was the popularization of country music—primarily, I think, by Johnny Cash and Glen Campbell; yet, as this book will remind you, relatively traditional ballads continued to attain great popularity, and anyway rock and the Nashville sound had deep roots in the musical past. Film became the hot new art form, as Hollywood died and the choking grip of studios, the star system and the money-making moguls was relaxed; but almost everybody alive today grew up with the movies, and now artists instinctively work in cinematic terms, even as audiences (readers, for instance) instinctively react to cinematic devices and influences. It is possible, nowadays, to see a movie exactly like the book it was made from, because the book was written in the first place by someone who did his learning at the movies and constructed his work out of that experience.

But far more traumatic forms of change were experienced in the Sixties, the most shaking of which may have been that many Americans—some of the most patriotic—came to believe that the national power somehow was out of control. The vast American war machine, which in the Eisenhower era they had learned to think of as a defense machine, and which they knew from a heritage aptly confirmed in World War II and Korea was *good* and even beneficial to oppressed mankind—the war machine became a menace, and not just to Cuba, the Dominican Republic, North Vietnam and the N.L.F., but to Americans and American society. The draft to man the machine, the funds to sustain it, the urge to use it, the controversy evoked among supporters and critics, the political power "defense" wielded over resources and priorities needed for other things, the corruption it fostered (the C.I.A. financing students, unions, foundations; the armed forces bribing Congressmen and reporters with junkets and preferment; contractors profiting from astronomical cost over-runs on contracts politically awarded; universities on the take)—all these brought power itself into disrepute, and the uses of power under sweeping challenge. And this happened even though, throughout the decade, the threat of world war seemed to rise steadily in the Middle East; and even though, in Czechoslovakia, the Soviet Union bluntly demonstrated its own power, its own brutal willingness to wield it.

The liberal faith also was shaken to its roots—not the political ideas, if any, of the so-called liberals of the two major parties, but the deepseated American belief in man's ability to "get together and work things out." That sort of ingrained rationalism had been seen in American institutions from the town meeting through the P.T.A. to collective bargaining. But in the Sixties—first—blacks lost whatever faith they had had in white intention to "work things out"; they began sitting in and burning down. Then white students, many of whom had gone to Mississippi in the early Sixties to teach illiterates and rebuild burned churches, and then had voted in 1964 for L.B.J. and against the war in Vietnam, discovered in action that "working within the system" was a slow and often fruitless task; they turned to mass demonstrations, draft resistance, campus strikes, building seizures. These "radical" actions, however the end seemed to justify the means, alarmed and outraged many other Americans— who abandoned *their* liberal faith in "working things out" by condoning or encouraging the sort of police violence loosed on white demonstrators at the Chicago national convention of the Democrats in 1968, or by acquiescing in various forms of "backlash" against black militants—electing reactionary officials, approving repressive action against the Black Panthers and others, opposing school integration, moving to the suburbs.

"What else could we do?" cried leaders on all sides, in the death rattle of liberal confidence, and in 1970, the whole action-reaction cycle of the Sixties came to a dreadful climax when the National Guard shot and killed four white demonstrators at Kent State, and Mississippi state police fired into a crowd of black students at Jackson State, killing two and wounding eleven. Another commission was appointed.

The loss of faith in "working things out" changed the spirit of accommodation in American life—which had always had its exceptions, particularly racial—to one of hostility; no wonder that at the end of the decade Mr. Nixon felt it necessary to pledge he would "bring us together." Roughly, the division was the young, the black, and the poor—the welfare poor, not the low-income poor—against everyone else. But the lines were not really that rigid—some young people, like the "Okie from Muskogee," were more hostile than anyone to draft resistance, long hair, militant blacks, campus unrest; some older persons like Senator McCarthy saw in the student movement the salvation of "the spirit of America," and some whites of every class and age continued to support the newly militant black cause. A better line of demarcation lay, perhaps, between those who believed *on faith* in the beneficence of American life and attitudes, and those who believed *on the evidence they saw* that the American idea was being perverted by "manipulators" such as Lyndon Johnson and Dean Rusk, later Richard Nixon, by the white power structure, the military-industrial complex, and corrupted institutions such as universities doing "defense" research or labor unions excluding blacks from good jobs.

But the division went deeper than that, too, sprang more directly from *change* itself—from loss and growth and pain, sorrow and remembrance, bewilderment and anger, dreams gone wrong and myths demolished. Here is a cry from the American heart, clipped from the letters column of a Texas newspaper:

Dear Mr. Editor:
   A few ideas, as we travel back down through memory lane:
   If you are a native American, and you are old enough, you will probably remember when you never dreamed our country could ever lose; when you took for granted that women and the elderly and the clergy were to be respected; when you went to church and found spiritual food; when the clergy talked about religion; when a girl was a girl; when a boy was a boy, and when they liked each other.
   You will probably remember when taxes were only a nuisance; when you knew your creditors and paid your debts; when the poor were too proud to take charity; when the words "care," "concern," "poverty" and "ghetto" were ordinary words and not overworked; when there was no bonus on bastards; when you knew that the law meant justice, and you had a feeling of protection and appreciation at the sight of a policeman; when young fellows tried to join the Army and Navy, when songs had a tune; when you bragged about your home state and your home town, and when politicians proclaimed their patriotism.
   You will remember when clerks in stores tried to please you; when our government stood up for Americans anywhere in the world; when a man who went wrong was blamed, not his mother's nursing habits or his father's income; when everyone knew the difference between right and wrong; when you considered yourself lucky to have a good job, when you were proud to have one.
   You may remember when people expected less and valued what they had more; when riots were unthinkable, when you took it for granted that the law would be enforced and your safety protected; when our flag was a sacred symbol; when America was the land of the free and home of the brave.
   Do you remember when—or do you?

Of course, there never really was such an America as that, but the poignant final question may be the one that mattered most in the Sixties. No matter what your age or party or color, if you longed for that kind of Arcadian America, what was actually happening frightened and repelled you, and so you were likely to be ranged against those who were in the thick of the "movement"—whether it was a movement of blacks, students, peacelovers, "hippies" or feminists. George Wallace even created a kind of reverse "movement" out of all those who were against the other movements. Surely, The Beatles touched a profound truth when they sang
   ...yesterday, love was such an easy game to play,
   now I need a place to hide away—
   Oh I believe in yesterday.
In particular, the yesterday many Americans believed in—the shaping time of the older generations, who came to maturity with different desperations, born of Depression and World War II—*that* yesterday was not infused with the peculiar apocalypses of today, the contrapuntal horrors of nuclear annihilation, the "population bomb," environmental destruction. This fact alone was change of incalculable import. Marching in the streets of the Sixties was the first generation to grow up entirely in the knowledge that if man's life was threatened with extinction, the fault lay not as much in his stars as in his habits and achievements—the first generation to place highest importance on man's survival against himself, rather than on the expansion of his domain, and the first generation that had had to.

Hence, the singular fact that young people generally—particularly black young people—were not nearly so moved or enthralled as their elders by the landing on the moon; it was not the giant step for mankind that many of them thought most needed.

And what was to give them hope? Wherever they—and many others—saw bright promise in the decade, it was cut down. John Kennedy, the triumph of the test-ban treaty in his hand, the Bay of Pigs far behind, the tragedy of Vietnam in the unimaginable future—his brain shattered on a sunlit day in Dallas. John XXIII, the interim Pope whose generosity of spirit lit the world—how brief *his* time of inspiration. From the blacks, one by one, gunmen and the fates took Malcolm X, Medgar Evers, the great Martin King, so different, so alike in their steadiness of purpose, *free at last, free at last*—but not the people for whom they spoke and died. Robert Kennedy, the inheritor of a legend, torn between political instinct and a suffering heart—downed at a moment of hope, the victim of a strange uprooted boy who stood witness to a displaced, distraught world of tortured dreams and frightened men. In this progression of death and violence was the most discouraging change—as if heroes could no longer survive nor hope live in such a world.

But somewhere, there had to be the *roots* of change, on the strength of which it could flourish so wildly in such a strange, wounding decade. Some sought the reasons in permissive parents, Supreme Court decisions, liberal politics, failing patriotism, black movement "too far too fast." But the search for such scapegoat sources of trouble never made more convincing progress than the most doctrinaire young radicals did in their attempts to isolate the "manipulators" and conspirators they believed to be blocking the world from its ordained path to the Age of Aquarius. Certain black advances, notably in the use of public accommodations in the South and the opening of housing patterns elsewhere, may have led to more black agitation for even further social gains, for instance, but this was a minor cause of racial conflict in the Sixties, compared to the urban aftermath of that all but unnoticed phenomenon of the Fifties—the great black migration from the Southern countryside into the black ghettos of the North and California.

For my part, I trace the Sixties' tidal wave of change, the decade's pervasive impression of disaster impending, its twilight sense of eras dying, as well as its suggestion—Aquarius again—of a new and brilliant dawn, to even deeper and more profound change here in America. At the heart of the decade, if seems to me, were two forces:

Technological accomplishment so far-reaching as actually to alter the means by which man perceived and learned, actually to extend his environment to new planets while threatening his extinction on his own.

Economic development so sweeping as to render all but obsolete the material standards by which American society had been able to gauge itself—making poverty, for instance, an interest-group problem like farm prices, shifting the basic issue of politics from the standard of living to the quality of life, and raising for millions of young Americans the unprecedented problem of finding something useful to do with their lives.

It is not yet clear what technology has in store for us, but it seems to bear the seeds of a mass and unhuman sort of life, no matter what our wealth. Already Americans are jammed into huge urban masses, in which they live stacked upon one another in numbered cells in beehive apartment buildings, or in endlessly sprawling suburbs whose houses have the same deadly sameness as units from the production line. Already these modern Americans submit to being sealed into gigantic toothpaste tubes and hurled through the skies at incredible speeds, literally peas in a pod, and already, for reasons no one can explain, the speed is being whipped up to supersonic levels. Already creatures of shrinking dimensions drive to work on swarming eight-lane highways, where metal monsters reduce human drivers to dollsize; and someday, if electronics prosper as predicted, the highway itself will drive the cars. Everywhere man turns, from the classroom to the supermarket to Mission Control, he is being dwarfed by his own handiwork—hapless and driven in his zip-code world, among his reactors and data banks, breathing his canned or polluted air and eating his frozen foods, even his physical security dependent—he is assured—upon the reaction time and judgment of an ABM computer. How typical and pathetic it was that when the great power failure of 1965 deprived urban Americans for a night of their greatest technological prop, human nature instinctively asserted itself in the darkness, and more children were conceived in and out of wedlock than on any other single occasion of which we have records on our ubiquitous punch cards.

Yet, the great impact of technology and affluence in the Sixties derived not only from what they did to American life but from what they did not do. When men were put on the moon by the aerospace industry and the "systems engineer," financed by a government bemused by political rivalry with the Soviet Union, the question was also raised in many an American mind why the same quality of effort and organization, the same level of financing, could not be brought to bear on, say, the housing problem or the transportation crisis. If technology could bounce the image of Richard Nixon off Telstar to Afghanistan, why could it not dispose of industrial waste without turning rivers purple and skies black? Why were superhighways easier to build for middle-class drivers than mass transit systems for the urban poor?

Somewhat similarly, it has to be supposed that if wealth is suddenly commonplace, after having been spread more widely than in any society in history, that fact will at some point make insistent the question why wealth can't be spread further—why, for instance, in the richest nation ever dreamed of, children still go hungry by the miserable thousands, and politicians can find nothing more to do about it than distribute surplus potatoes and food stamps designed mostly to make certain the poor can't buy TV sets or bottles of cheap wine or otherwise undermine their own moral fiber?

Almost subversively, in the Sixties, technology and affluence thus betrayed institutions and ethics based on an older, different order of things. They helped produce, for instance, the issue of "relevance" or lack of it in American education. A generation reared before the TV set, blasé about computer technology, unimpressed by the glories and dangers of the past (as compared to those of the Sixties in America), and with little if any concern about money, found the university not only a stuffy place but its wares unexciting and seemingly not very useful in the social cause. Billions of dollars annually, technically augmented firepower, and computer-run pacification programs could neither win the war in Vietnam nor convince Americans it was necessary, much less an exercise of benevolent power.

Before the possibilities raised by technology and affluence, moreover, it became apparent that the home political system had all but broken down. Organized fundamentally for the needs of the Nineteenth Century, divided into fifty historical accidents, each of *them* subdivided with stultifying effect into outmoded, inefficient, underfinanced, overlapping, jealous and innumerable smaller jurisdictions, this antiquated system channeled the lion's share of tax revenues to its swollen central government, which was therefore expected to provide an impossible variety and scope of activities, for most of which it has small understanding or aptitude; but the population was concentrated in cities that had no appreciable powers of government and no revenue sources but the most unproductive and unfair.

And what kind of political, economic and technological society was it that could spawn the monstrous Rayburn Building on Capitol Hill and the F-111 in Fort Worth and the whiz-kid systems analysts of Robert McNamara (the spoiled priest of a technological god that failed) and still not be able to collect the garbage in New York City or protect old ladies walking their dogs or place any useful restriction on the nation's ninety million privately owned firearms?

By the end of the Sixties, it was thus becoming reasonably clear that the United States of America, rich and ingenious as it might be, simply was not organized to cope with the Twentieth Century or to do the things its affluence and technology made possible; and those born too far along in this breakdown of the American system to defend it blindly and on faith seemed more and more justified in their mistrust of its workings and claims.

Failing institutions, moreover, mean failing ethical standards. When government, local or national, cannot restrain the violence of its own agents, preaching non-violence to radicals and blacks will not have much effect. Veneration for the Presidency cannot long be sustained if the occupants of that office too often are caught misleading or mistrusting the people. Political rhetoric about the glories of the nation's history will sound the more hollow as it is used to respond to those who point out present deficiencies.

And where affluence and technology are so pervasive, what is—for example—the sense of continuing to emphasize the old values of primitive, pioneer America—hard work, iron self-discipline, personal material success, the primacy of productivity? Particularly if conformity to those values is made the only norm of respectability and social acceptability, the ethic itself can only seem the more irrelevant, the conformity the more choking.

Recently, a man of some distinction told me that he was glad he had grown to manhood years ago, at a time when it not only was possible but probably was necessary for him to erect a material standard by which to measure his life. It had been possible for him to judge the worth of his labors, over the years, by asking how much he had been able to ease the physical difficulties of his family, increase the prosperity of his society, conquer the technical obstacles to abundance for all. But in the age of affluence and technology, he said, no such simple material standard could suffice. Wealth had become the general rule and the gross national product dwarfed the wildest dreams; miracles were commonplace, and men could survive even with other men's hearts pumping their blood, at the bottom of the sea and in the great void of space, by the mere technological expedient of carrying their environment with them. Every day, another of man's limitations fell away.

As for affluence, then, what is to be its net worth? What kind of lives shall we live and what values shall we profess and what rich rewards of the mind and spirit are we to seek, with means and leisure and the advantages they afford? Accumulation itself, as a goal and certainly as a value, is satisfying, if at all, only to those who accumulate from need, and material overachievement can have no more utility than nuclear overkill.
What value can be erected in its stead?

And as for technology, are we going to use it in a reasoned way to improve the lot of man, materially, spiritually, intellectually, in his environment, or are we going to become technology's slaves—as seems dreadfully possible—mounting each new scientific Everest not because it serves man's purpose but merely because it is there?

On how we come to use our affluence and technology and the things they afford us, it is not too much to say, depends the question whether Americans of today and tomorrow, born in a new world and reared in its influences, can find something that *they will regard as useful to do with their lives in their times.* Building a better mousetrap lost its essential appeal once it ceased to mean a more craftsmanlike piece of work and suggested, instead, trickier packaging and louder advertising; and the extension of built-in obsolescence (not excluding that of human beings who become progressively less employable after 40) throughout the Gross National Product marks the extent to which the old material standard defrauds rather than measures honest value. Social involvement, personal intellectual or esthetic development, environmental preservation, back-to-nature communes, public services, the constructive use of leisure—all these and other callings plainly offer more nearly a pioneer challenge today than the business successes, industrial feats and financial wizardries that once sang their siren songs to young Americans.

So I believe we have now to turn away from the gods of production that for so long comforted us, as we measured ourselves against their demands; I think the Sixties—*change* —taught, if we would learn, that we have before us the task of making a tolerable life in a new and difficult world no less than did those who came centuries ago to the wild shores of America in search of freedom and opportunity. But that task will demand of us primarily a sense of value, not the material standard that served them; it will require us to believe, with Thoreau, that the world is more to be admired than used; that our lives are more to be cultivated and contemplated than driven and exploited; that the only true progress is within ourselves, toward the only true value—the old enduring values of the human heart, courage and pity and joy and the generosities of love.

Oh when will you ever learn? sang the young people of the Sixties, in their innocence, their green ignorance of the small daily deaths of the spirit that life itself—not some political or economic system—deals to the great and the small. *When will we ever learn?* It was hard to live in the music and clangor of the Sixties without asking that question. In their echoes, in an America changing from a lusty boomer's youth to maturity or decline, it is even harder to believe in Arcadia or Aquarius. *When will we ever learn?* After the Sixties, perhaps as never before, the answer, my friend, is blowin' in the wind; the answer is blowin' in the wind.

Tom Wicker
June, 1970

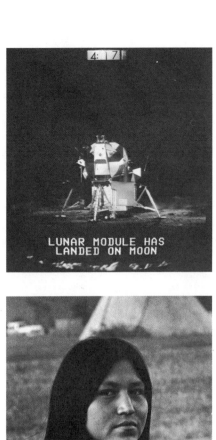

18

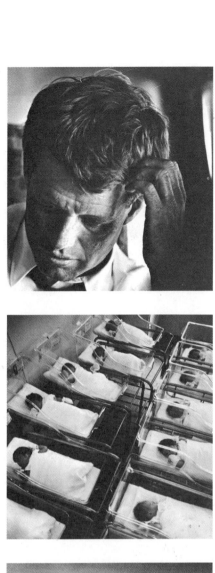

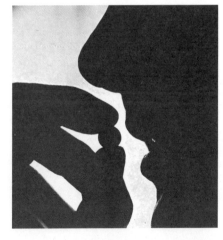

  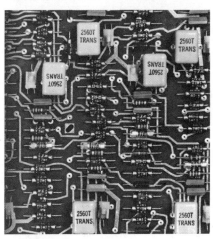

Alfie

Words by Hal David
Music by Burt Bacharach

Very Slowly, Rubato

sure   as   I   be - lieve   there's   a   heav - en   a -

bove,   Al - fie,   I   know   there's some - thing much

more,   some - thing e - ven   non - be - liev - ers   can   be - lieve   in.

I   be - lieve in love,   Al - fie._____   With - out true love we just ex -

Angel Of The Morning

Words and Music by Chip Taylor

I see no need to take me home, I'm old e-nough to face the dawn.
And if we're vic-tims of the night, I won't be blind-ed by the light.

Just call me An - gel__ Of The Morn - ing,__ (an - gel) just touch my cheek be-fore you

leave me, ba - by. Just call me An - gel__ Of The Morn - ing,__ (an - gel)

then slow-ly turn a-way from me.

then slow-ly turn a-way,

rubato

a tempo

rubato

I won't beg you to stay with me,_____ through the tears

of the day,_____ of the years.

Ba - by,_____ ba - by, ba - by Just call me An - gel _____ Of The

Morn - ing,_____ (an - gel) just touch my cheek be - fore you leave me, ba - by.

Repeat and Fade

By The Time I Get To Phoenix

Words and Music by Jimmy Webb

Last time
To Coda

1.

2. By the

Blowin' In The Wind

Words and Music by Bob Dylan

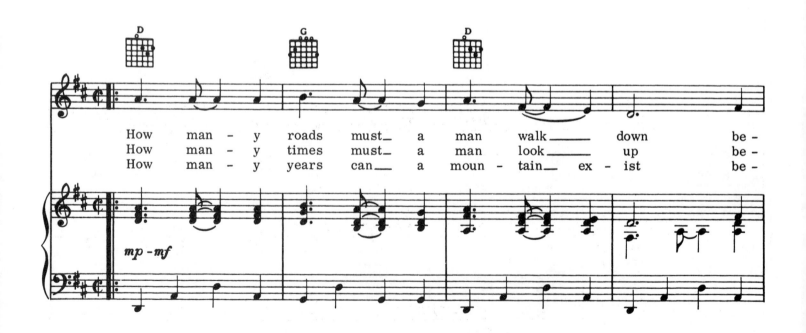

How	man - y roads must a man walk down	be -
How	man - y times must a man look up	be -
How	man - y years can a moun - tain ex - ist	be -

Bridge Over Troubled Water

Words and Music by Paul Simon

I will lay me down. _____

Sail on

sil - ver girl,   Sail on   by.

From the Musical CABARET

Cabaret

Words by Fred Ebb
Music by John Kander

Life is a Cab - a - ret, old chum,

Come to the Cab - a -

ret._____ ret. Come taste the

wine, Come hear the band, Come blow the

From the Paramount Picture THE STERILE CUCKOO

Come Saturday Morning (Saturday Morning)

Words by Dory Previn
Music by Fred Karlin

Creeque Alley

Words and Music by John Phillips and Michelle Gilliam

1. John and Mitch - ie were
2. - ly said, "Den - ny, you know __
3.-5. *See additional lyrics*

get - tin' kind of itch - y just to leave the folk mu - sic be - hind.
__ there aren't man - y who can sing a song the way that you do. __

__ Let's go __ south." Zal and Den - ny work -
Den - ny says, "Zal - ly, gol - ly,

Additional Lyrics

3. When Cass was a sophomore,
planned to go to Swarthmore,
but she changed her mind one day.
Standin' on the turnpike
thumb out to hitchhike,
take her to New York right away.
When Denny met Cass he gave her love bumps,
called John and Zal and that was the Mugwumps.
McGuinn and McGuire couldn't get no higher,
but that's what they were aimin' at,
and no one's gettin' fat except Mama Cass.

4. Mugwumps, high jumps, slow slumps, big bumps.
Don't you work as hard as you play?
Make-up, break-up, ev'rything you shake up,
guess it had to be that way.
Sebastian and Zal formed a Spoonful;
Michelle, John and Denny gettin' very tuneful.
McGuinn and McGuire just a-catchin' fire.
In L.A. you know where that's at.
And everybody's gettin' fat except Mama Cass.
Do do do do do do, do do do do, woh.

5. Broke, busted, disgusted, agents can't be trusted;
and then she wants to go to the sea.
Cass can't make it. She says, "We'll have to fake it."
We knew she'd come eventually.
Greasin' on American Express card,
Tents, low rent and keepin' out the heat's hard
Duffy's good vibrations and our imaginations
can't go on indefinitely,
and California Dreamin' is becoming a reality.

Dancing In The Street

Words and Music by Marvin Gaye, Ivy Hunter and William Stevenson

Moderately, with a steady beat

57

The Dangling Conversation

Words and Music by Paul Simon

now late aft - er - noon,_____ As the
I my Rob - ert Frost,_____ And we
words that must be said,_____ 'Can an -

sun shines through the cur - tained lace _____ and
note our place with book mark - ers _____ that
al - y - sis be worth - while?'_____ 'Is the

sha - dows wash the room. _____
meas - ure what we've lost. _____
thea - ter real - ly dead?'_____

And we sit and drink our cof - fee _____
Like a po - em poor - ly writ - ten _____ we are
Now the room is soft - ly fad - ed _____ and I

couched in our in - dif - fer - ence, like shells up - on the shore You can
ver - ses out of rhy - thm, _____ coup - lets out of rhyme, in _____
on - ly kiss your sha - dow, I can - not feel your hand, You're a

hear the o - cean roar _____ in the
syn - co - pat - ed time _____ and the
strang - er now un - to me _____ lost in the

Dang-ling Con-ver-sa-tion _____ and the sup-er-fi-cial

sighs _____ {the / are the / in the} bord-ers of our lives. _____

1. 2.

3.

2. And you _____
3. Yes, we

8va bassa

Different Drum

Words and Music by Michael Nesmith

love _____ on - ly me. _____ Yes, and

I ain't say - in' you ain't pret - ty, all I'm say - in's

I'm not read - y for an - y per - son, place or thing ___ to

try and pull ___ the reins ___ in on me.

Do You Believe In Magic

Words and Music by John Sebastian

makes you feel hap-py like an old time mov-ie. I'll tell you 'bout the mag-ic and it'll

free your soul But it's like try-in' to tell a stran-ger 'bout a rock and roll.____

2. If you be-lieve in mag - ic   don't you both-er to choose, If it's
3.(If you be-lieve in mag)-ic   come a-long with me. We'll____

jug band__ mu - sic or rhy - thm and blues, Just go and lis - ten, it - 'll
dance un - til morn - ing 'til there's just you and me And may - be ba - by if the

start with a smile that won't wipe off your face no mat - ter
mu - sic is right. I'll___ meet you to - mor - row and we'll

how hard you try. Your feet start tap - pin' and you can't seem to find How you
go late at night. And we'll go danc - in' ba - by then___ you'll see How the

Downtown

Words and Music by Tony Hatch

noise and the hur - ry seems to help, I know.___ Down - town. Just
plac - es to go___ to where they nev - er close.___ Down - town. Just
* And

list - en to the mu - sic of the traf - fic in the ci - ty.
list - en to the rhy - thm of a gen - tle Bos - sa No - va.
you may find some - bod - y kind to help and un - der stand you.

Ling - er on the side - walk where the ne - on signs are pret - ty.
You'll be danc - ing with 'em too be - fore the night is ov - er,
Some - one who is just like you and needs a gen - tle hand to

Eleanor Rigby

Words and Music by John Lennon and Paul McCartney

Moderately, with a steady beat

Ah _____ look at all _____ the lone - ly peo -

- ple! _____ Ah _____ look at all _____

_____ the lone - ly peo - ple! _____

who   is   it   for?
what   does   he   care?
no   one   he   was   saved.

All   the   lone - ly   peo -

- ple,   where do____ they all____ come from?____

All   the   lone - ly   peo - ple,   where do____ they all____ be - long?____

To Coda

1. D.C. al Coda

2.

Coda

76

From MIDNIGHT COWBOY

Everybody's Talkin' (Echoes)

Words and Music by Fred Neil

Moderately

mf

mp

Eve-ry-bod-y's   Talk-in' at me   I don't hear a   word they're say-in'

On-ly the ech-oes___ of my   mind._____   Peo-ple

stop-pin' star-in' I can't see the fac-es On-ly the sha-dows__ of their

eyes._____ I'm go-in' where the sun__ keeps shin-in'

thru the pour-in' rain Go-in' where the wea-ther__ suits my

clothes_____ Bank-in' off of the north-east wind Sail-in' on a sum-mer

breeze _____ Skip-pin' o-ver the o-cean like a stone. _____

Eve-ry-bod-y's Talk-in' at me I don't hear a word they're say - in'

On - ly the ech-oes _____ of my mind. _____ And

Repeat and Fade

I won't let you leave my love _____ be-hind _____ No,
I won't let you leave my love _____ be-hind _____ And,
I won't let you leave my love _____ be-hind. _____

Eve Of Destruction

Words and Music by P.F. Sloan

1. The East - ern world _ it is ex - plod - in',
3., 4. *See additional lyrics*

vi - o - lence flar - in' and bul - lets load - in'. You're old e - nough to kill, but

not for _ vot - in', You don't be - lieve in war, but what's that gun you're to - tin'? And

MCA Music Publishing

2. Don't you un - der - stand what I'm try'n to say?__ Can't you feel the fear__ that I'm

feel - in' to - day? If the but - ton is pushed __ there's no

run - ning a - way._____ There'll be no one to save__ with the

world in a grave. __ Take a look a - round you, boy, it's

Additional Lyrics

3. My blood's so mad feels like coagulatin'
   I'm sittin' here just contemplatin'
   You can't twist the truth it knows no regulatin'
   And a handful of Senators don't pass legislation
   Marches alone can't bring integration
   When human respect is disintegratin'
   This whole crazy world is just too frustatin'.
   (To Chorus:)

4. Think of all the hate there is in Red China
   Then take a look around to Selma, Alabama!
   You may leave here for four days in space
   But when you return, it's the same old place,
   The pounding drums, the pride and disgrace
   You can bury your dead, but don't leave a trace
   Hate your next door neighbor, but don't forget to say grace.
   (To Chorus:)

Gentle On My Mind

Words and Music by John Hartford

2. It's not clinging to the rocks and ivy planted on their columns now that binds me
   Or something that somebody said because they thought we fit together walkin'.
   It's just knowing that the world will not be cursing or forgiving when I walk along
   Some railroad track and find
   That you're moving on the backroads by the rivers of my memory and for hours
   You're just gentle on my mind.

3. Though the wheat fields and the clothes lines and junkyards and the highways
   Come between us
   And some other woman crying to her mother 'cause she turned and I was gone.
   I still run in silence, tears of joy might stain my face and summer sun might
   Burn me 'til I'm blind
   But not to where I cannot see you walkin' on the backroads by the rivers flowing
   Gentle on my mind.

4. I dip my cup of soup back from the gurglin' cracklin' caldron in some train yard
   My beard a rough'ning coal pile and a dirty hat pulled low across my face.
   Through cupped hands 'round a tin can I pretend I hold you to my breast and find
   That you're waving from the backroads by the rivers of my memory ever smilin'
   Ever gentle on my mind.

Goin' Out Of My Head

Words and Music by Teddy Randazzo and Bobby Weinstein

Slowly, with a beat

Well I think I'm go - ing out of my head.
(And I) think I'm go - ing out of my head.

Yes I think I'm go - ing out of my head o - ver
'Cause I can't ex - plain the tears that I shed o - ver

you o - ver you I
you o - ver you I

From GEORGY GIRL

Georgy Girl

Words by Jim Dale
Music by Tom Springfield

lone - li - ness there   in - side you. Hey there!__

Geor - gy Girl,__

1. Why do all the boys just pass you by?
2. Dream-ing of the some - one you could be.

Could it be you just don't try, or is it the clothes you wear?__
Life is a re - al - i - ty, you can't al - ways run a - way.__

The Girl From Ipanema

(Garôta De Ipanema)

English Words by Norman Gimbel
Original Words by Vinicius de Moraes
Music by Antonio Carlos Jobim

Moderately

Tall and tan and young_ and {love - ly, The Girl___ / hand - some, the boy___} From I - pa - ne- - ma goes walk - ing, and when__ {she pass - es, each one__ she / he pass - es, each girl__ he} pass - es goes

Hey Jude

Words and Music by John Lennon and Paul McCartney

I Want To Hold Your Hand

Words and Music by John Lennon and Paul McCartney

Oh yeh, I'll _____ tell you some - thing I think you'll un - der-

stand. Then I'll _____ say that some - thing,

I Want To Hold Your Hand.___ I Want To Hold Your

Hand._____ I Want To Hold Your Hand. Oh ___

please ___ say to me ___ and let me be your

man, and please ___ say to me ___

love I can't hide,___ I can't hide,___ I can't hide.___

Yeh, you _____ got that

some - thing, I think you'll un - der - stand. When

I _____ {say}{feel} that some - thing, I Want To Hold Your Hand,___

I Can See For Miles

Words and Music by Peter Townshend
Bright Rock

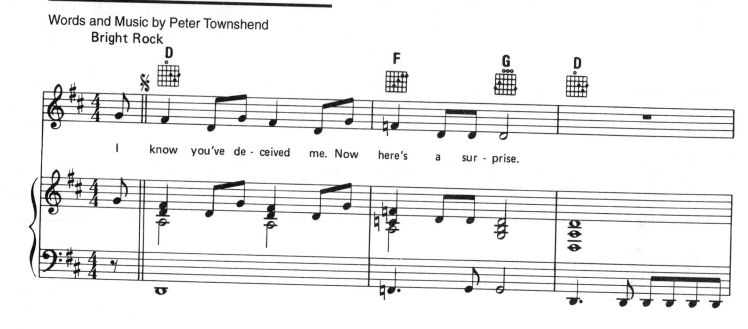

I know you've de - ceived me. Now here's a sur - prise.

I know that you have 'cos there's ma - gic in____ my

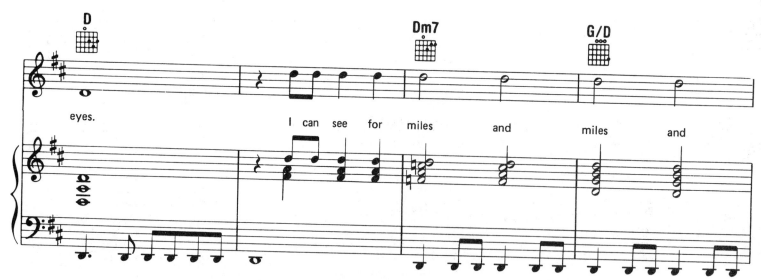

eyes. I can see for miles and miles and

109

From THE UMBRELLAS OF CHERBOURG

I Will Wait For You

Music by Michel Legrand
Original French Text by Jacques Demy
English Lyrics by Norman Gimbel

Interlude

clock will tick a - way the hours one by one ____ and then the time will come when all the wait - ing's done. ____ The time when you re - turn and find me here and run, ____ Straight to my wait - ing arms. _____ 3. If it

114

In The Ghetto (The Vicious Circle)

Words and Music by Mac Davis

And his ma-ma cries. _____ 'Cause if

there's one thing that she _____ don't need _____ it's an-oth-er hun-gry mouth _____ to feed _____ In The

Ghet-to. _____ Peo-ple, don't you un-der-stand _____ the child needs a

help-ing hand _____ or he'll grow to be an an-gry young man some day. Take a look at

119

If I Were A Carpenter

Words and Music by Tim Hardin

If I_ Were A Car-pen-ter_ and you were a la-dy
If I_ worked my hands in wood_ would you still_ love me?_

_ Would you mar-ry me an-y-way, Would you have my ba-by?_
_ An-swer me,_ Babe, "Yes I would, I'd put you a-bove me."_

If a tink-er were my trade,_ would you still love me?_
If I were a mill-er at a mill wheel grind-ing,_

Car - ry - ing the pots I made,___ fol - low - ing be - hind me.___
Would you miss your col - ored box,___ your soft shoes shin - ing?___

Save my love through lone - li - ness,___ Save my love for sor - row I've giv - en you my

own - li - ness___ Come and give me your to - mor - row.___

mor - row.___

If You Go Away

French Words and Music by Jacques Brel
English Words by Rod McKuen

new and our hearts were high; When the day was young___ and the night___ was
love with-out lov-ing you; Can I tell you now,___ as you turn___ to
look I see on your face, I'd have been the shad-ow of your shad-ow if

long, And the moon stood still___ for the night-bird's song.⎫
go, I'll be dy-ing slow-ly till the next hel-lo. ⎬ If you go a-
I thought it might have kept me by your side.⎭

way, if you go a - way, if you go a - way, if you go a - way. But if you
(Last time) please don't go a - way. But if you
Fine

stay, I'll make you a day, Like no day has been, or will be a-
stay, I'll make you a night, Like no night has been, or will be a-

1. Ne me quitte pas,
   Il faut oublier
   Tout peut s'oublier
   Qui s'enfuit déjà,
   Oublier le temps
   Des malentendus
   Et le temps perdu
   A savoir comment
   Oublier ces heures
   Qui tuaient parfois
   A coups de pourquoi
   Le coeur du bonheur...
   Ne me quitte pas,
   Ne me quitte pas,
   Ne me quitte pas,
   Ne me quitte pas.

2. Moi je t'offrirai
   Des perles de pluie
   Venues de pays
   Ou il ne pleut pas;
   Je creusrai la terre
   Jusqu'après me mort
   Pour couvrir ton corps
   D'or et de lumière;
   Je f'rai un domaine
   Ou l'amour s'ra roi
   Ou l'amour s'ra roi
   Ou tu seras reine
   Ne me quitte pas,
   Ne me quitte pas,
   Ne me quitte pas,
   Ne me quitte pas.

3. Ne me quitte pas,
   Je t'inventerai
   Des mots insenses
   Que tu comprendras,
   Je te parlerai
   De ces amants là
   Qui ont vû deux fois
   Leurs coeurs s'embraser,
   Je te racont'rai
   L'histoire de ce roi
   Mort de n'avoir pas
   Pu te rencontrer
   Ne me quitte pas,
   Ne me quitte pas,
   Ne me quitte pas,
   Ne me quitte pas.

4. On a vu souvent
   Rejaillir le feu
   De l'ancien volcan
   Qu'on croyait trop vieux;
   Il est, parait-il,
   Des terres brulées
   Donnant plus de blé
   Qu'un meilleur avril,
   Et quand vient le soir
   Pour qu'un ciel flamboie
   Le rouge et le noir
   Ne s'epous'nt ils pas
   Ne me quitte pas,
   Ne me quitte pas,
   Ne me quitte pas,
   Ne me quitte pas.

5. Ne me quitte pas,
   Je n'vais plus pleurer
   Je n'vais plus parler,
   Je me cach'rai la
   A te regarder
   Causer et sourire
   Et a t'écouter
   Chanter et puis rire;
   Laiss'moi de venir
   L'ombre de ton ombre,
   L'ombre de ta main,
   L'ombre de ton chien;
   Ne me quitte pas,
   Ne me quitte pas,
   Ne me quitte pas,
   Ne me quitte pas.

From MAN OF LA MANCHA

The Impossible Dream (The Quest)

Lyric by Joe Darion
Music by Mitch Leigh

Is That All There Is

Words and Music by Jerry Leiber and Mike Stoller

bears... and a beautiful lady in pink tights flew high above our heads... as I sat there watching

the marvelous spectacle... I had the feeling that something was missing... I don't know what, but when it

N.C.

was over... I said to myself, "Is that all there is to the circus?" *Sung:* Is that all there is? _

Fm9   Abm6   Fm9

Spoken: Then I fell in love... head over heels in love with the most wonderful { boy / girl } in the world...

we would take long walks by the river, or just sit for hours gazing into each others eyes...

we were so very much in love.... then one day... { he / she } went away... and I

thought I'd die... but I didn't... and when I didn't I said to myself, "Is that all

there is to love? *Sung:* Is that all there is? _____

It Was A Very Good Year

Words and Music by Ervin Drake

small town girls and soft sum-mer nights,_____ We'd
cit - y girls who lived up the stair, _____ With
blue - blood-ed girls of in - de-pen-dent means,_____ We'd
vin - tage wine from fine old kegs, _____ From the

hide from the lights_____ on the
per - fumed hair _____ that
ride in li - mou - sines _____ their chauf-
brim to the dregs_____ it

vil - lage green _____ When I was
came un - done _____ When I was
feurs would drive_____ When I was
poured sweet and clear, _____ It was a

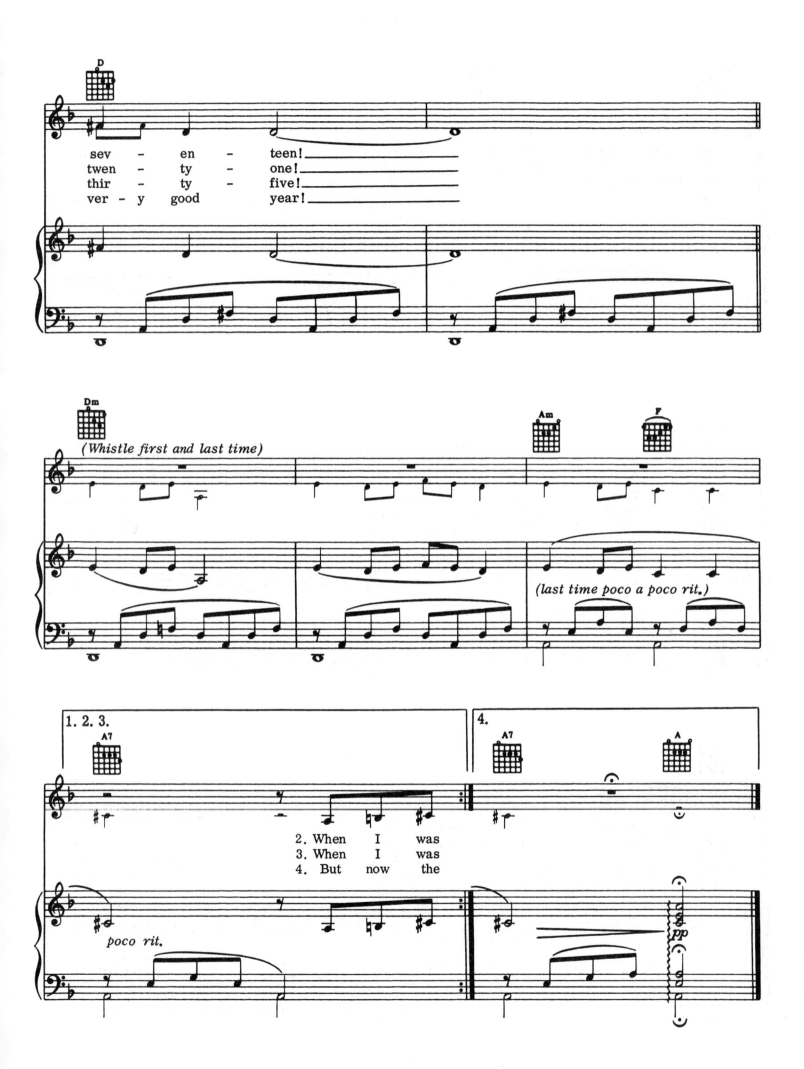

King Of The Road

Words and Music by Roger Miller

I ain't got no ci - ga - rettes.__ Ah, but   two hours__ of
I don't pay no un - ion dues.__ I smoke   old sto - gies
I ain't got no ci - ga - rettes.__ Ah, but   two hours__ of

push - ing broom__ Buys a   eight__ by twelve__ four - bit room.__ I'm a
I have found,__   Short__ but not too big a - round.__ I'm a
push - ing broom__ Buys a   eight__ by twelve__ four - bit room.__ I'm a

man   of   means by   no means,   King__ Of The

1. Road.

2. Road.   To next strain   2. I know

3. Road.   Fine

ev - er - y en - gi - neer on ev - er - y train.

All of the chil - dren and all of their names__ And

ev - er - y hand - out in ev - er - y town__ And

ev - 'ry lock that ain't locked when no one's a - round. 3. I sing

D.S. al Fine 𝄇

142

The Last Thing On My Mind

Words and Music by Tom Paxton

2. As we walk, all my thoughts are a-tumblin',
   'Round and 'round, 'round and 'round.
   Underneath our feet the subway's rumblin',
   Underground, underground.

   (Chorus)

3. You've got reasons a-plenty for goin',
   This I know, this I know.
   For the weeds have been steadily growing,
   Please don't go, please don't go.

   (Chorus)

4. As I lie in my bed in the morning,
   Without you, without you.
   Each song in my breast dies a-borning,
   Without you, without you.

   (Chorus)

Leaving On A Jet Plane

Words and Music by John Denver

lone - some I ___ could ___ cry. _____
{bring} your wed - ding ___ ring. _____
{wear}
I won't have ___ to ___ say. _____

Chorus

So kiss me and smile for me, ___ Tell me that ___ you'll

wait for me, ___ Hold me like ___ you'll nev-er let me go. ___

149

The Look Of Love

Words by Hal David
Music by Burt Bacharach

Medium Rock Ballad (with much feeling)

A Lover's Concerto

Words and Music by Sandy Linzer and Denny Randell

Birds high up - on the trees ser - e - nade the

flow'rs with their mel - o - dies. Oh, _____ see there be - yond the

hill, the bright col - ors of the rain - bow.

Some mag - ic from a - bove made this day for

155

Love Is All Around

Words and Music by Reg Presley

From MAME

Mame

Music and Lyric by Jerry Herman

With a lilt

You coax the blues right out__ of the horn, Mame,____
You've brought the cake-walk back__ in-to style, Mame,____

You charm the husk right off__ of the corn, Mame,____
You make the weep-in' wil-lowtree smile, Mame,____

You've got the ban-joes strum-min' and plunk-in' out a tune to beat the
Your skin is Dix-ie sat-in, there's reb-el in your man-ner and your

band,
speech,
The whole plan - ta - tion's hum - min' since
You may be from Man - hat - tan, but

you brought Dix - ie back to Dix - ie - land.
Geor - gia nev - er had a sweet - er peach.
You make the
You make our

cot - ton eas - y to pick,
black - eyed peas_ and our grits,
Mame,____
Mame,____
You give my
Seem like the

old mint ju - lep a kick,
bill of fare_ at the Ritz,
Mame,____
Mame,____
You make the
You came, you

161

Monday, Monday

Words and Music by John Phillips

Moderately

mf

1, 3. Mon - day, Mon - day,   so good_ to me_
2. Mon - day, Mon - day,   Can't trust_ that day_

Mon - day morn - in', it_ was all_ I hoped it would
Mon - day, Mon - day, some - times it just turns out that

be._____ Oh, Mon - day morn - in', Mon - day morn-

way._____ Oh, Mon - day, morn - in' you give me no warn-

\- in' could-n't guar - an - tee_____ That Mon - day

\- in' ___ of what was to be ___ Oh, Mon - day,

eve - nin' you would still be here___ with me.

Mon - day how could you leave and not ___ take

2.

Ev-'ry oth-er day,_____ ev-'ry

oth-er day, ev-'ry oth-er day of the week is fine, yeah!_____

But when-ev-er Mon-day comes, but when-ev-er Mon-day comes you can find me

cry'n, yeah!_____

D.S. and fade

165

From A MAN AND A WOMAN

A Man And A Woman (Un Homme Et Une Femme)

Original Words by Pierre Barouh
English Words by Jerry Keller
Music by Francis Lai

Moderately

When hearts are pass-ing in the night, In the lone-ly night___
si-lence of the mist, Of the morn-ing mist___

Then they must hold each oth-er tight, Oh so ver-y tight___
When lips must are wait-ing to be kissed, Long-ing to be kissed.___

And take a chance that in the light In to-mor-row's light___
Where is the rea-son to re-sist And de-ny a kiss___

They'll stay to - geth - er_____ So much in love. And in the
That holds a prom - ise_____ Of hap - pi - ness.

Tho yes - ter - day_____ still sur - rounds you___ With a warm and
pre - cious mem - o - ry._____ May - be_____ for to - mor - row___
_____ we can build a new dream____ for you and me. This glow we

feel is some-thing rare, Some-thing real-ly rare_____ So come and
pass-ing in the night, In the rush-ing night_____ A man, a

say you want to share want to real-ly share_____ the beau-ty
wo-man in the night, In the lone-ly night_____ Must take a

wait-ing for us there, Call-ing for us there_____ that on-ly
chance that in the light, In to-mor-row's light_____ they'll be to-

lov-ing_____ can give the heart. When life is
geth-er_____ so much in

Tacet

From JACQUES BREL IS ALIVE AND WELL AND LIVING IN PARIS

Marieke

Original Words by Jacques Brel
English Words by Eric Blau
Original Music by Jacques Brel and Gerard Jouannest

Zon-der liefde wa-arm de liefde___ Lijdt het licht, het don-ker licht,___
Zon-der liefde wa-arm de liefde___ Lijdt het licht, tout est fi - ni___

En schuurt de zand o - ver mijn land, Mijn plat-te land mijn Vlaan-deren land.
En schuurt het zand o - ver mijn land, Mijn plat-te land mijn Vlaan-deren land.

Ay, Ma - rie - ke, Ma - rie - ke, the bells have rung,

the e - choes sound, the day is done. Ay, Ma - rie-ke, Ma - rie-ke,

in Flan-ders field,   the e-choes sound,   the day is gone.

Zon-der liefde wa-arm de liefde__   Lacht de duivel, de zwar-te duivel.__

Zon-der liefde, wa-arm-de liefde__   Brandt mijn hart, mijn ou-de hart__

Zon-der liefde, wa-arm-de liefde__   Sterft de zomer de droe-ve zomer__

En schuurt het zand-o-ver mijn land, Mijn plat-te land mijn Vlaan-deren-land.

Ay, Ma-rie-ke, Ma-rie-ke, come back a-gain, come back a-gain,

The day is gone, Ay, Ma-rie-ke, Ma-rie-ke,

Your love a-lone, your love a-lone, the day is gone.

Mellow Yellow

Words and Music by Donovan Leitch

Moderately slow, with a "Rock" beat

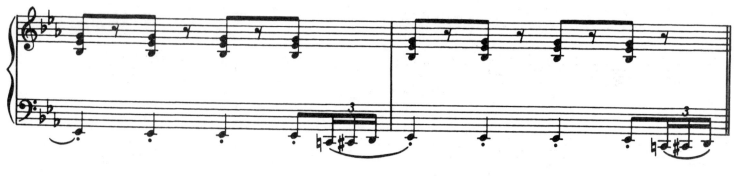

I'm just mad a-bout Saf - fron,___ A - Saf - fron's mad a-bout me;___
I'm just mad a-bout Four - teen,___ A - Four - teen's mad a-bout me;___
Born__ high for ev-er to___ fly,___ A - wind-a ve - loc-i-ty nil;___

179

From the Paramount Picture BREAKFAST AT TIFFANY'S

Moon River

Words by Johnny Mercer
Music by Henry Mancini

af - ter the same rain - bow's end _____

_____ wait - in' 'round the bend, _____ my Huck - le - ber - ry

friend, Moon Riv - er _____ and

1. me. _____

2. me. _____

rall. _____

Mr. Tambourine Man

By Bob Dylan

jin-gle jan-gle morn-in' I'll come fol - low-in' you.

Verse

1. Though I know that eve-nin's em - pire has re-turned in - to sand,

Van-ished from my hand, Left me blind-ly here to stand but still not

sleep-in'! My wea-ri-ness a - maz-es me I'm

184

brand - ed on my feet. I have no one to meet And the

an - cient emp - ty street's too dead for dream - in'. _____

Repeat 3 times

(Chorus)

2. Take me on a trip upon your magic swirlin' ship
   My senses have been stripped, my hands can't feel to grip
   My toes too numb to step, wait only for my boot heels
   To be wanderin'
   I'm ready to go anywhere, I'm ready for to fade
   Into my own parade, cast your dancin' spell my way
   I promise to go under it.

(Chorus)

3. Though you might hear laughin' spinnin' swingin' madly across the sun
   It's not aimed at anyone, it's just escapin' on the run
   And but for the sky there are no fences facin'
   And if you hear vague traces of skippin' reels of rhyme
   To your tambourine in time, it's just a ragged clown behind
   I wouldn't pay it any mind, it's just a shadow you're
   Seein' that he's chasin'.

(Chorus)

4. Then take me disappearin' through the smoke rings of my mind
   Down the foggy ruins of time, far past the frozen leaves
   The haunted, frightened trees out to the windy beach
   Far from the twisted reach of crazy sorrow
   Yes, to dance beneath the diamond sky with one hand wavin' free
   Silhouetted by the sea, circled by the circus sands
   With all memory and fate driven deep beneath the waves
   Let me forget about today until tomorrow.

(Chorus)

Mrs. Robinson

Words and Music by Paul Simon

Look a-round you, all_ you see_ are sym-pa-thet-ic eyes,_____

D.S. ℅

Stroll a-round_ the grounds_ un-til you feel at home._ And here's to you,_

Coda ⊕

Verse

2. Hide it in a hid - ing place_ where no one ev-er goes,_
3. Sit - ting on a so - fa on_ a Sun-day af - ter-noon,_

_____ Put it in your pant - ry with_ your cup-
Go - ing to the can - di - dates' de-bate,_

cakes,_____

It's a lit-tle se-cret, just__ the Rob-

Laugh a-bout it, shout__ a-bout__ it,_____

in-son's af-fair,_____ Most_____ of all,

When you've got__ to choose,_____ Ev-'ry way you__ look__

you've got to hide___ it from the kids.___ Coo, coo, ca-choo,___

at it,___ you lose. Where have you gone___

Chorus

Mrs. Rob-in son,___ Je-sus loves you more__ than you__ will

Joe Di-mag-gi-o?___ A na-tion turns its__ lone-ly eyes__ to

My Cherie Amour

Words and Music by Stevie Wonder, Sylvia Moy and Henry Cosby

193

From Jules Dassin's Motion Picture NEVER ON SUNDAY

Never On Sunday

Words by Billy Towne
Music by Manos Hadjidakis

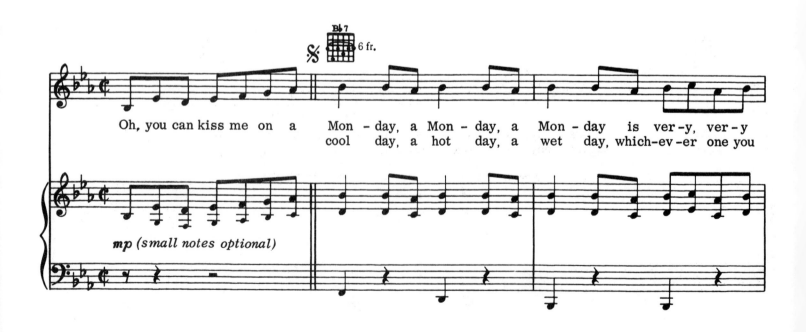

Oh, you can kiss me on a Mon-day, a Mon-day, a Mon-day is ver-y, ver-y
cool day, a hot day, a wet day, which-ev-er one you

say, _____ but my day of rest.

Just name the day _____ that you like the

best, _____ On - ly stay a - way _____

_____ on my day of rest.

Tacet

D. S. al Fine 𝄋

Oh, you can kiss me on a

New York Mining Disaster 1941

Words and Music by Barry Gibb and Robin Gibb

seen my wife, Mis-ter Jones? Do you know what it's like on the

out-side? Don't go talk-ing too loud, you'll cause a land-slide, Mis-ter

To Coda ⊕

Jones. I keep strain-ing my ears to hear a sound, may-be

some-one is dig-ging un-der-ground. Or have they giv-en up and all gone home to

199

bed think-ing those who once ex-ist-ed must be dead. Have you

seen my wife, Mis-ter Jones? Do you know what it's like on the out-side? Don't go

talk-ing too loud, you'll cause a land-slide, Mis-ter Jones.

D.S. al Coda

In the e -

Coda

Jones.

200

Quiet Nights Of Quiet Stars (Corcovado)

English Words by Gene Lees
Original Words and Music by Antonio Carlos Jobim

MCA Music Publishing

From ON A CLEAR DAY YOU CAN SEE FOREVER

On A Clear Day (You Can See Forever)

Words by Alan Jay Lerner
Music by Burton Lane

you are. On A Clear Day

How it will as - tound you That the

glow of your be - ing out - shines ev - 'ry

star. You feel part of ev - 'ry

mf piú espr.

205

On Broadway

Words and Music by Barry Mann, Cynthia Weil, Mike Stoller and Jerry Leiber

Papa's Got A Brand New Bag

Words and Music by James Brown

From FUNNY GIRL

People

Words by Bob Merrill
Music by Jule Styne

Lov-ers_____ are ver-y spec-ial peo-ple,_____ They're the
luck - i - est peo - ple_____ in the world._____
With one per - son,_____ One ver - y spe - cial
per - son,_____ A feel - ing deep in your soul_____ Says: you were

half, now you're whole._____ No more hun-ger and thirst, But

first, be a per-son who needs peo - ple._____ Peo - ple who need

peo - ple_____ Are the luck-i-est peo - ple in the

1. world._____ 2. world._____

People Got To Be Free

Words and Music by Felix Cavaliere and Edward Brigati, Jr.

Bright Rock

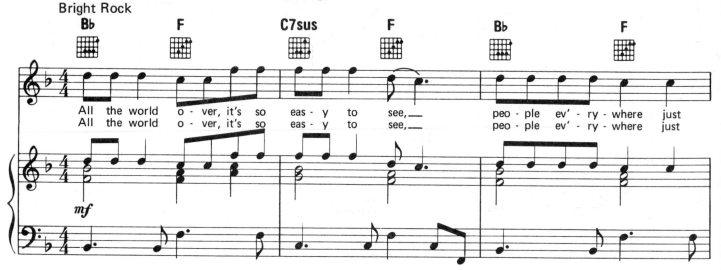

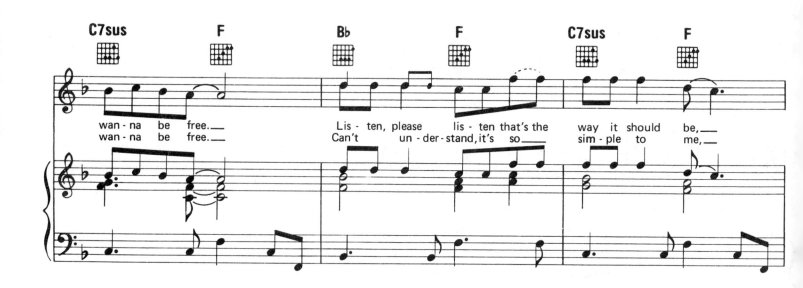

220

Ask me my o-pin-ion, my o-pin-ion will be,___ it's a nat-'ral sit-u-a-tion for a
Ev'-ry-bod-y's danc-in', come on let's___ go see,___ there's_ peace_ in the val-ley, now we

man to be free.___
all can be free.___

Spoken: Look, see that train over there? Now
You know it's been long over -

that's the train of freedom, it's about to arrive any minute now.
due, Look out 'cause it's comin' right on through.

Repeat and Fade

221

Raindrops Keep Fallin' On My Head

Lyric by Hal David
Music by Burt Bacharach

Moderate, Rhythmically

Rain - drops Keep Fall - in' On My Head, and

just like the guy whose feet are too big for his

Reason To Believe

Words and Music by Tim Hardin

D.S. al Fine

San Francisco (Be Sure To Wear Some Flowers In Your Hair)

Words and Music by John Phillips

To Coda ⊕

In the streets___ of San Fran - cis - co,___
If you come___ to San Fran - cis - co,___

Gen - tle peo - ple___ with flow - ers in their
Sum - mer time ___ will be a love - in

hair._____

All a-cross the na - tion,___

231

232

Society's Child

Words and Music by Janis Ian

Come to my door, baby,
Walk me down to school, baby,
One of these days I'm gon-na stop my list-'ning,

Face is clean and shin-ing black as night,
Ev-'ry bod-y's act-ing deaf and dumb,
Gon-na raise my head up high,

My moth-er went to
Un-til they turn and
One of these days I'm gon-na

an-swer you know that you looked so fine.
say, "Why don't you stick to your own kind."
raise up my glis-ten-ing wings and fly.

Now
My

The Sound Of Silence

Words and Music by Paul Simon

sleep - ing,   And the vi - sion _____ that was plant - ed   in my   brain _____

_____ still re - mains _____   with - in The Sound   Of   Si - lence. _____

2. In rest - less dreams I walked a - lone   nar - row streets of cob - ble -
3. And in the nak - ed light I saw   ten thou - sand peo - ple may - be

stone,   'neath the ha - lo of a   street   lamp, _____
more.   Peo - ple talk - ing with - out   speak - ing, _____

I turned my col - lar to the cold and damp___   When my eyes were stabbed___
___ peo-ple hear-ing with-out lis - ten-ing___   Peo - ple writ - ing songs___

___ by the flash of a ne - on light   that split the night___
___ that voi - ces___ nev - er share   and no one dare___

___ and touched The Sound   Of Si - lence.___
___ dis - turb The Sound   Of Si - lence.___

(4.) "Fools!" said I "You do not know   si-lence like a can - cer grows.

Hear my words that I might teach you,___ Take my arms that I might

reach you."___ But my words___ like si-lent rain-drops fell,

and ech-oed___ in the wells of si-lence.___

(5.) And the peo-ple bowed and prayed to the ne-on god they made.

Stop! In The Name Of Love

Words and Music by Lamont Dozier, Brian Holland and Edward Holland

Spinning Wheel

Words and Music by David Clayton Thomas

247

Adapted from A MAN COULD GET KILLED

Strangers In The Night

Words by Charles Singleton and Eddie Snyder
Music by Bert Kaempfert

Moderately slow

Stran - gers In The Night _____ ex - chang - ing glanc - es,

won - d'ring in the night _____ what were the chanc - es

MCA Music Publishing

we'd be shar - ing love_____ be - fore the night was

through._____ Some -thing in your eyes_____

_____ was so in - vit - ing, some - thing in your smile_____

_____ was so ex - cit - ing, some - thing in my heart_____

250

love was just a glance a-way, a warm em-brac-ing dance a-way and

ev-er since that night_____ we've been to-geth - er, lov-ers at first sight_____

_____ in love for-ev - er. It turned out so right_____ for Stran-gers In The

1. Night.

2. Night._____

Suzanne

Words and Music by Leonard Cohen

cra - zy   and that's   why   you want to   be   there;   And she
cer - tain   on - ly   drown - ing men   could   see Him   He
hon - ey   on our   la   -   dy   of   the   har - bour;   And she

Em   F

feeds you   tea and   o -ran-ges   that came all   the way from   Chi - na,   And
said "All   men shall be   sail - ors,   then, un - til   the sea   shall   free them,"   But
shows you where to   look a - mid   the   gar -bage and   the   flow -ers.   There are

C

just when you   want to   tell her_____   that   you have   no love   to give her_____   she
He   Him-self was   bro -ken long   be -fore   the sky   would o - pen._____   For -
he - roes in   the   sea-weed,_____   There are chil - dren in   the morn-ing,_____   they are

gets you on her wave length and lets the riv-er an-swer that you've
sak - en, al - most hu - man, He sank be-neath your wis - dom like a
lean-ing out for love, and they will lean that way for - ev - er while

al - ways____ been her lov - er.____ And you
stone._____ And you
Suz - anne____ holds her mir-ror.____ And you

Chorus

want to trav - el with her,____ And you want to trav - el blind,_____ And you
want to trav - el with Him,____ And you want to trav - el blind,_____ And you
want to trav - el with her,____ And you want to trav - el blind,_____ And you

think you may - be trust her,___ 'Cause she's touched your per-fect bod-y,___ with her
think you may - be trust Him,___ For he's touched your per-fect bod-y,___ with His
think may-be you'll trust her,___ For you've touched her per-fect bod-y,___ with your

1.2.

mind.___
mind.___

2. And
3. Suz -

3.

mind.___

ritard

From NO STRINGS

The Sweetest Sounds

Lyrics and Music by Richard Rodgers

What do I real- ly hear_____ And what is in the ear of my mind?

Which sounds are true and clear_____ And which will nev-er be de- fined?

The sweet- est sounds I'll ev- er

hear Are still in- side my head.____

____ The kind- est words I'll ev- er

know Are wait- ing to be said.____

____ The most en- tranc- ing sight of

all is yet for me to see.____

Those Were The Days

Words and Music by Gene Raskin

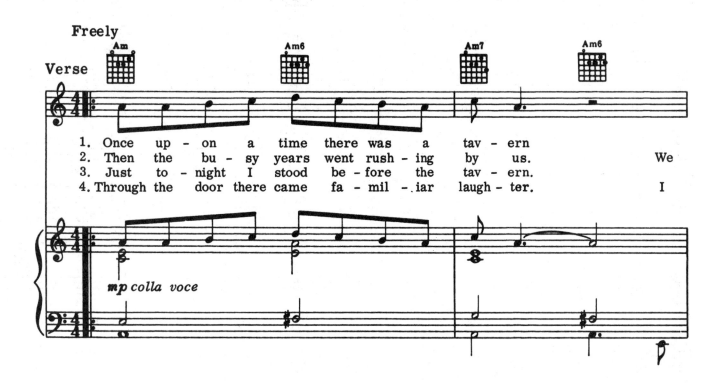

1. Once up-on a time there was a tav-ern
2. Then the bu-sy years went rush-ing by us.
3. Just to-night I stood be-fore the tav-ern.
4. Through the door there came fa-mil-iar laugh-ter.

Where we used to raise a glass or two,
lost our star-ry no-tions on the way.
Noth-ing seemed the way it used to be.
saw your face and heard you call my name.

Re-mem-ber how we laughed a-way the
If by chance I'd see you in the
In the glass I saw a strange re-
Oh my friends we're old-er but no

Chorus

hours,   And dreamed of   all   the great things we would do.   Those Were The
tav-ern,   We'd smile   at   one an-oth-er   and we'd say   Those Were The
flec-tion.   Was   that   lone-ly fel-low real-ly me?   Those Were The
wis-er,   For   in   our hearts the dreams are still   the same.   Those Were The

A Tempo

Days,   my friend.__ We thought they'd nev-er   end,__ We'd sing and dance   for-

ev-er and a   day;   We'd live the   life   we   chose,__ We'd fight and

From the Paramount Picture ROMEO AND JULIET

A Time For Us (Love Theme)

Words by Larry Kusik and Eddie Snyder
Music by Nino Rota

Slowly and Very Expressively

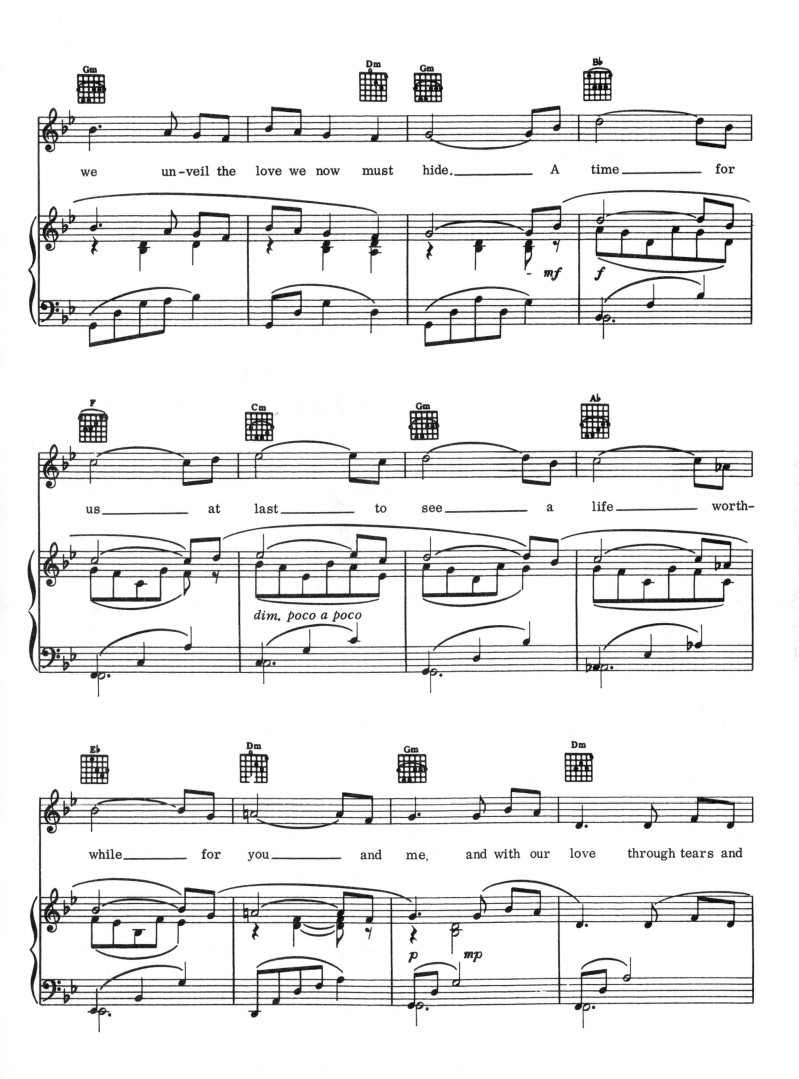

The Times They Are A-Changin'

By Bob Dylan

1. Come gath-er 'round peo-ple where-ev-er you roam _____ And ad-mit that the wa-ters a-round you have

grown And ac - cept it that soon you'll be drenched to the

bone,_____ If your time to you is worth sav - in'_____

_____ Then you bet - ter start swim-min' or you'll sink like a

stone, For The Times They Are A - Chang -

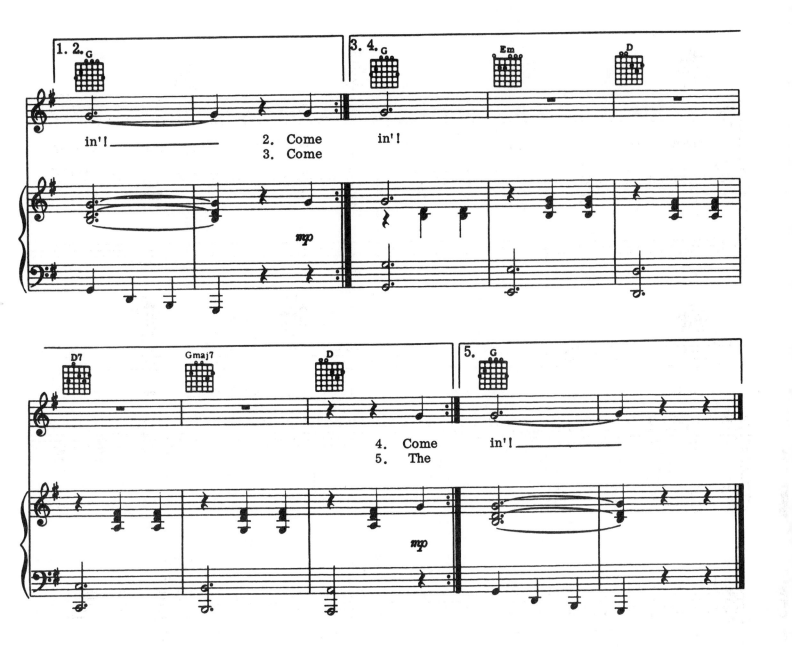

in'! _____   2. Come   in'!
3. Come

4. Come   in'! _____
5. The

2. Come writers and critics
   Who prophesies with your pen
   And keep your eyes wide
   The chance won't come again.
   And don't speak too soon
   For the wheel's still in spin
   And there's no tellin' who
   That it's namin'
   For the loser now
   Will be later to win
   For the times they are a-changin'.

4. Come mothers and fathers,
   Throughout the land
   And don't criticize
   What you can't understand.
   Your sons and your daughters
   Are beyond your command
   Your old road is
   Rapidly agin'
   Please get out of the new one
   If you can't lend your hand
   For the times they are a-changin'.

3. Come senators. congressmen
   Please heed the call
   Don't stand in the doorway
   Don't block up the hall.
   For he that gets hurt
   Will be he who has stalled
   There's a battle
   Outside and it's ragin'
   It'll soon shake your windows
   And rattle your walls
   For the times they are a-changin'.

5. The line it is drawn
   The curse it is cast
   The slow one now will
   Later be fast.
   As the present now
   Will later be past
   The order is rapidly fadin'
   And the first one now
   Will later be last
   For the times they are a-changin'.

From THE FANTASTICKS

Try To Remember

Words by Tom Jones
Music by Harvey Schmidt

Up, Up And Away

Words and Music by Jimmy Webb

Turn! Turn! Turn!
(To Everything There Is A Season)

Words from the Book of Ecclesiastes
Adaptation and Music by Pete Seeger

Verse

2. A time to build up, a time to break down;
   A time to dance, a time to mourn;
   A time to cast away stones,
   A time to gather stones together.

3. A time of love, a time of hate;
   A time of war, a time of peace;
   A time you may embrace,
   A time to refrain from embracing.

4. A time to gain, a time to lose;
   A time to rend, a time to sew;
   A time to love, a time to hate;
   A time for peace, I swear it's not too late.

From JACQUES BREL IS ALIVE AND WELL AND LIVING IN PARIS

La Valse à Mille Temps (Carousel)

Original Words and Music by Jacques Brel
English Words by Eric Blau

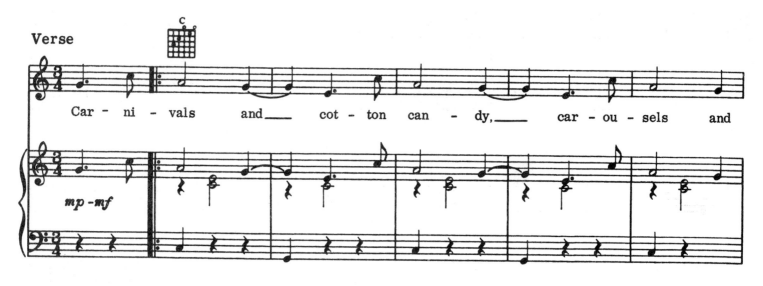

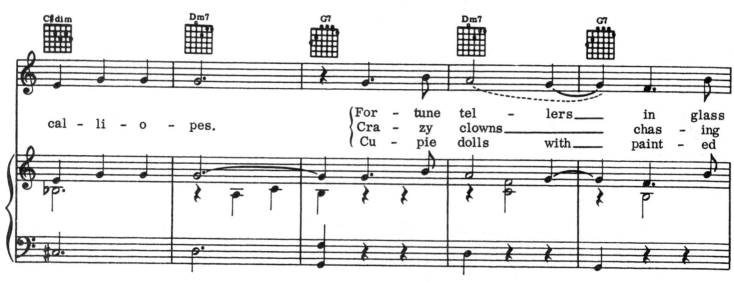

Waist Deep In The Big Muddy

Words and Music by Pete Seeger

knee deep in the Big Mud – dy but the
big fool said to push on. _____ (2. The) _____

2. The sergeant said, "Sir, are you sure,
   This is the best way back to base?"
   "Sergeant, go on; I forded this river
   'Bout a mile above this place
      It'll be a little soggy but just keep slogging.
      We'll soon be on dry ground."
      We were waist deep in the Big Muddy
      And the big fool said to push on.

3. The sergeant said, "Sir, with all this equipment
   No man'll be able to swim."
   "Sergeant, don't be a nervous Nellie,"
   The Captain said to him.
      "All we need is a little determination;
      Men, follow me, I'll lead on."
      We were neck deep in the Big Muddy
      And the big fool said to push on.

4. All at once, the moon clouded over,
   We heard a gurgling cry.
   A few seconds later, the Captain's helmet
   Was all that floated by.
      The sergeant said, "Turn around men,
      I'm in charge from now on."
      And we just made it out of the Big Muddy
      With the Captain dead and gone.

5. We stripped and dived and found his body
   Stuck in the old quicksand
   I guess he didn't know that the water was deeper
   Than the place he'd once before been.
      Another stream had joined the Big Muddy
      'Bout a half mile from where we'd gone.
      We were lucky to escape from the Big Muddy
      When the big fool said to push on.

6. Well, I'm not gonna point any moral;
   I'll leave that for yourself
   Maybe you're still walking and you're still talking
   And you'd like to keep your health.
      But every time I read the papers
      That old feeling comes on;
      We're waist deep in the Big Muddy
      And the big fool says to push on.

7. Waist deep in the Big Muddy
   And the big fool says to push on
   Waist deep in the Big Muddy
   And the big fool says to push on
      Waist deep! Neck deep!
      Soon even a tall man'll be over his head
      Waist deep in the Big Muddy!
      And the big fool says to push on!

Walk On By

Lyric by Hal David
Music by Burt Bacharach

With a beat

1. If you see me walk-in' down the street and I start to cry___
2. I just can't get o-ver los-in' you and so if I seem___

each time we meet,___ ⎫
bro-ken and blue,___ ⎭ Walk On   By,___

Walk on by, ____

{ Make be - lieve ____ that
{ Fool - ish pride, ____ that's

you don't see the tears, Just let me grieve ____ in
all that I have left, So let me hide ____ in the

pri - vate, 'Cause each time I see you, I break down and
tears and the sad - ness you gave me when you said good-

285

We Shall Overcome

Musical and Lyrical Adaptation by Zilphia Horton, Frank Hamilton, Guy Carawan and Pete Seeger
Inspired by African American Gospel Singing, members of the Food and Tobacco Workers Union, Charleston, SC, and the southern Civil Rights Movement

day, _____ Oh, _____ deep in my
day, _____ Oh, _____ deep in my

heart   I   do   be - lieve
heart   I   do   be - lieve

We   Shall   O - ver   come   some   day. _____
We   Shall   O - ver   come   some

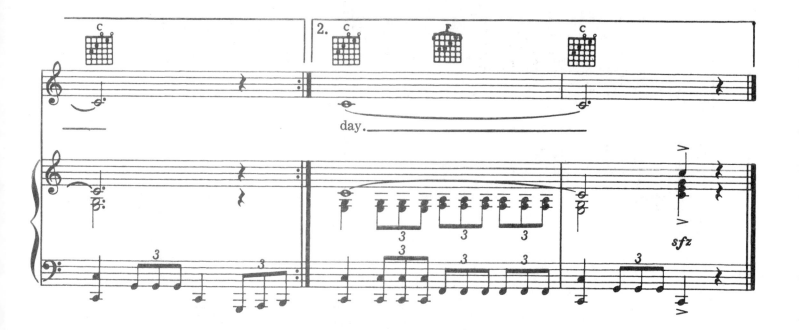

day.

3. We are not afraid, we are not afraid,
    We are not afraid today,
    Oh, deep in my heart I do believe
    We shall overcome some day.

4. We shall stand together, we shall stand together,
    We shall stand together – now,
    Oh, deep in my heart I do believe
    We shall overcome some day.

5. The truth will make us free, the truth will make us free,
    The truth will make us free some day.
    Oh, deep in my heart I do believe
    We shall overcome some day.

6. The Lord will see us through, the Lord will see us through,
    The Lord will see us through some day,
    Oh, deep in my heart I do believe
    We shall overcome some day.

7. We shall be like Him, we shall be like Him,
    We shall be like Him someday,
    Oh, deep in my heart I do believe
    We shall overcome someday.

8. We shall live in peace, we shall live in peace,
    We shall live in peace some day,
    Oh, deep in my heart I do believe
    We shall overcome some day.

9. The whole wide world around, the whole wide world around,
    The whole wide world around some day,
    Oh, deep in my heart I do believe
    We shall overcome some day.

10. We shall overcome, we shall overcome,
    We shall overcome some day,
    Oh, deep in my heart I do believe
    We shall overcome some day.

We'll Sing In The Sunshine

Words and Music by Gale Garnett

Moderately slow

We'll sing in the sun - shine, _____ we'll laugh ev - 'ry day; _____

we'll sing in the sun - shine _____ and I'll be on my way.

I will nev - er love ____ you; _____ the cost of love's too dear. ____
sing to you each morn - ing, _____ I'll kiss you ev - 'ry night. __
dad - dy, he once told ____ me, _____ don't love you an - y { man,
                                                                { wo -
when our year has end - ed _____ and I have gone a - way, __

What Now My Love

(Original French Title: "Et Maintenant")

Original French Lyric by Pierre Delanoe
Music by Gilbert Becaud
English Adaptation by Carl Sigman

Moderate Bolero Tempo

What Now My Love_____ Now that you left me_____ How can I
Love_____ Now that it's o - ver_____ I feel the

live_____ through an - oth - er day_____ Watch-ing my
world_____ clos - ing in on me_____ Here come the

dreams_____ Turn - ing to ash - es_____ And my
stars_____ Tum - bling a - round me_____ There's the

hopes_____ in - to bits of clay_____ Once I could
sky_____ where the sea should be_____ What Now My

see_____ Once I could feel_____ Now I am
Love_____ Now that you're gone_____ I'd be a

numb   I've be – come   un – real _____   I walk the
fool   to go   on   and   on _____   No one would

night _____   With – out a   goal _____   Stripped of my
care _____   No one would   cry _____   If I should

heart, _____   my   soul. _____   What Now My
live _____   or   die. _____

What The World Needs Now Is Love

Lyric by Hal David
Music by Burt Bacharach

World Needs Now Is Love, sweet love,

No, not just for some,_____ but for ev-'ry-one._____

Lord, we don't need an-oth-er moun-tain,_____ There are
Lord, we don't need an-oth-er mead-ow,_____ There are

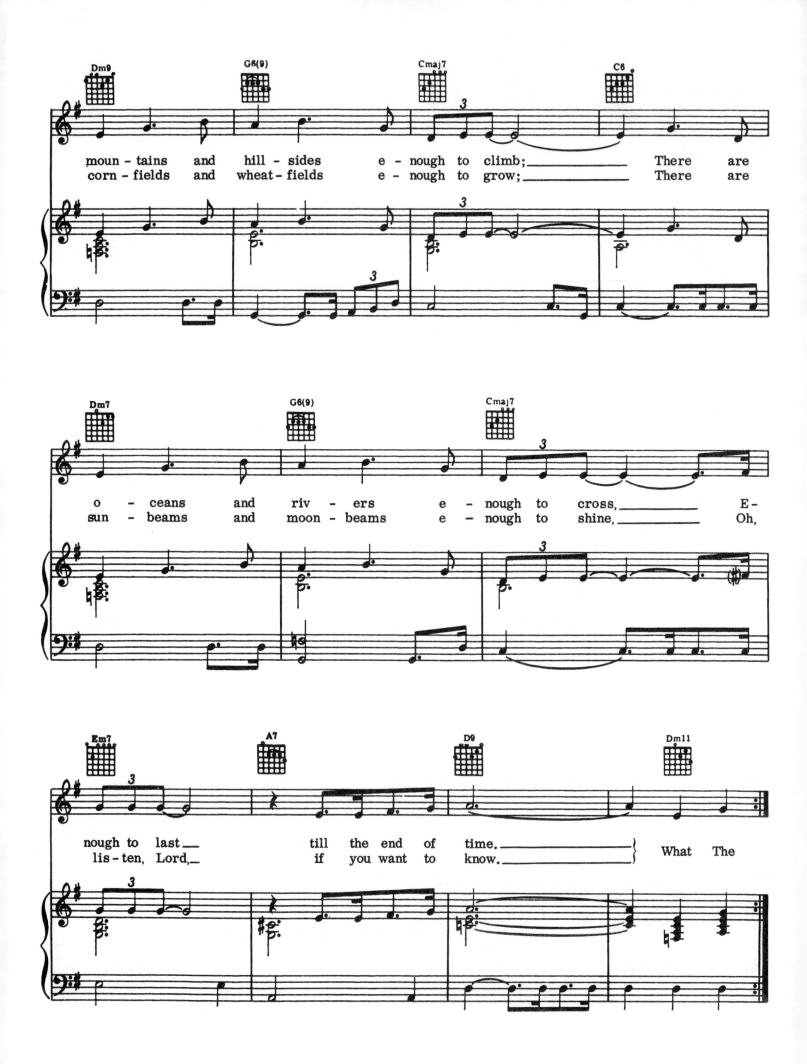

moun-tains and hill-sides e-nough to climb;_____ There are
corn-fields and wheat-fields e-nough to grow;_____ There are

o-ceans and riv-ers e-nough to cross,_____ E-
sun-beams and moon-beams e-nough to shine,_____ Oh,

nough to last___ till the end of time.___ What The
lis-ten, Lord,___ if you want to know.___

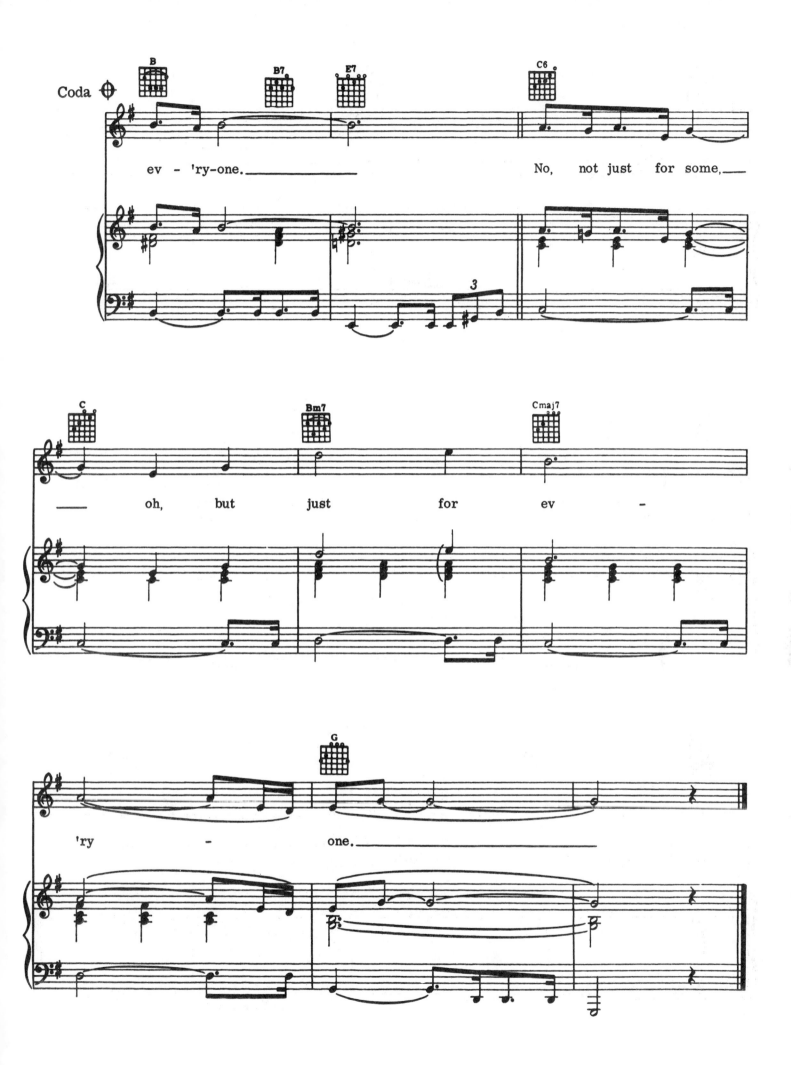

You Keep Me Hangin' On

Words and Music by Edward Holland, Lamont Dozier and Brian Holland

me but you keep   me hang - in' on. _____
me you just keep   me hang - in' on. _____

Why do ___ you keep a com-in' a - round _ play - ing with my heart? _

_____ Why don't _ cha get out ___ of my life _____

and let me make a new start? _ Let me get o - ver you _ the

way you've got-ten o - ver me. _____ You say ___ al - though ___

we ___ broke up ___ you still wan - na be just friends.

But how can we still ___ be friends ___ when see - ing you on - ly breaks my

heart a - gain? ___ *(Spoken:)* *And there ain't nothing I can do about it.*

You've Lost That Lovin' Feelin'

Words and Music by Barry Mann, Cynthia Weil and Phil Spector

You've Really Got A Hold On Me

Words and Music by William "Smokey" Robinson

Slowly

311

Tight - er

Yesterday

Words and Music by John Lennon and Paul McCartney

I said some-thing wrong now I long for yes-ter-day.

Yes-ter-day, love was such an eas-y game to play

Now I need a place to hide a-way__ Oh I be-lieve__ in

yes-ter-day.__ Mm mm mm mm mm.__

316

Milton Okun

Milton Okun, legendary record producer, arranger, and founder of Cherry Lane Music Company, was born in New York City. He received his BS in Music Education from New York University, his Masters of Education from the Oberlin Conservatory of Music and taught music in the New York City public school system early in his career.

Among his numerous and varied associations, Okun was the arranger and conductor for Harry Belafonte, and the arranger and producer for Peter, Paul and Mary, as well as the Chad Mitchell Trio, before embarking on his historic association with John Denver as producer, musical director and publisher. Among Okun's prized recordings are those with Placido Domingo. Okun was also the arranger of the classic collection, "The Compleat Beatles," and has earned 46 gold and platinum records.

Tom Wicker

Tom Wicker joined the New York Times's Washington Bureau in 1960, becoming Bureau Chief four years later. He authored the Times's "In The Nation" column from 1996 until his retirement in 1991.

Born in Hamlet, North Carolina, Wicker never lost his love for down-home music, and as the father of two children, had considerable exposure to it, both live and on records. His essay in this book, "Arcadia and Aquarius," encapsulates his keen observations of the changing times of the Sixties.

great songs...

This legendary series has delighted players and performers for generations!

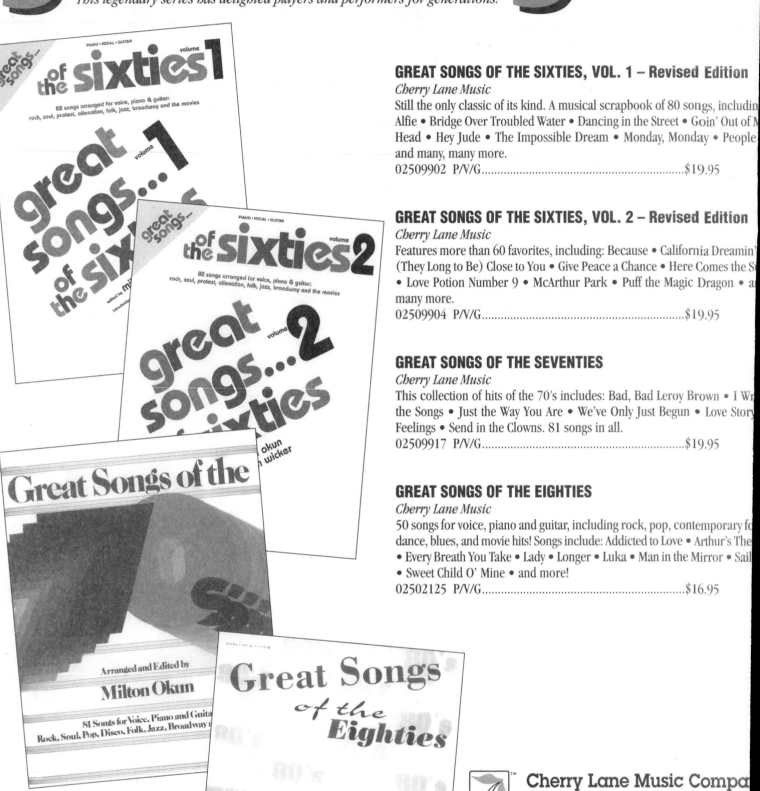

GREAT SONGS OF THE SIXTIES, VOL. 1 – Revised Edition
Cherry Lane Music

Still the only classic of its kind. A musical scrapbook of 80 songs, includin
Alfie • Bridge Over Troubled Water • Dancing in the Street • Goin' Out of M
Head • Hey Jude • The Impossible Dream • Monday, Monday • People
and many, many more.
02509902 P/V/G...$19.95

GREAT SONGS OF THE SIXTIES, VOL. 2 – Revised Edition
Cherry Lane Music

Features more than 60 favorites, including: Because • California Dreamin'
(They Long to Be) Close to You • Give Peace a Chance • Here Comes the S
• Love Potion Number 9 • McArthur Park • Puff the Magic Dragon • a
many more.
02509904 P/V/G...$19.95

GREAT SONGS OF THE SEVENTIES
Cherry Lane Music

This collection of hits of the 70's includes: Bad, Bad Leroy Brown • I Wr
the Songs • Just the Way You Are • We've Only Just Begun • Love Story
Feelings • Send in the Clowns. 81 songs in all.
02509917 P/V/G...$19.95

GREAT SONGS OF THE EIGHTIES
Cherry Lane Music

50 songs for voice, piano and guitar, including rock, pop, contemporary fo
dance, blues, and movie hits! Songs include: Addicted to Love • Arthur's The
• Every Breath You Take • Lady • Longer • Luka • Man in the Mirror • Sail
• Sweet Child O' Mine • and more!
02502125 P/V/G...$16.95

Cherry Lane Music Compa
• Quality In Printed Music •
6 East 32nd Street, New York, NY 100

FOR MORE INFORMATION, SEE YOUR LOCAL MUSIC DEALER,
OR WRITE TO:

HAL•LEONARD®
CORPORATION
7777 W. BLUEMOUND RD. P.O. BOX 13819 MILWAUKEE, WI 53213

Prices, contents and availability subject to change without notice.
Some products may not be available outside the U.S.A.